Faith *of the*
First Ladies

Other books by Jerry MacGregor and Marie Prys

1001 Surprising Things You Should Know
    about the Bible

1001 Surprising Things You Should Know
    about Christianity

1001 Surprising Things You Should Know
    about God

Faith *of the* First Ladies

Jerry MacGregor
and Marie Prys

BakerBooks
Grand Rapids, Michigan

© 2006 by Jerry MacGregor and Marie Prys

Published by Baker Books
a division of Baker Publishing Group
P.O. Box 6287, Grand Rapids, MI 49516-6287

Printed in the United States of America

All rights reserved. No part of this publication may be reproduced, stored in a retrieval system, or transmitted in any form or by any means—for example, electronic, photocopy, recording—without the prior written permission of the publisher. The only exception is brief quotations in printed reviews.

Library of Congress Cataloging-in-Publication Data
MacGregor, Jerry.
    Faith of the First Ladies / Jerry MacGregor and Marie Prys.
       p.   cm.
    Includes bibliographical references.
    ISBN 0-8010-6593-3 (pbk.)
    1. Presidents' spouses—Religious life—United States. 2. Presidents' spouses—United States—Biography. I. Prys, Marie. II. Title.
    E176.2.M23 2006
    973.09'9—dc22
                                 2005025389

Unless otherwise indicated Scripture is taken from the HOLY BIBLE, NEW INTERNATIONAL VERSION®. NIV®. Copyright © 1973, 1978, 1984 by International Bible Society. Used by permission of Zondervan. All rights reserved.

Scripture marked NRSV is taken from the New Revised Standard Version of the Bible, copyright 1989, Division of Christian Education of the National Council of the Churches of Christ in the United States of America. Used by permission. All rights reserved.

Scripture marked NASB is taken from the New American Standard Bible®, Copyright © 1960, 1962, 1963, 1968, 1971, 1972, 1973, 1975, 1977, 1995 by The Lockman Foundation. Used by permission.

Permission to publish the poems "The Open Door" and "Watch-Fires," written by Grace Coolidge, graciously given by the Calvin Coolidge Memorial Foundation, Inc., P.O. Box 97, Plymouth, VT 05056.

For Tom Day, who inspired me to write, and Helen Bateman, who encouraged me to be better than I was. Great teachers change lives. You both changed mine.

CHIP

For my sisters—Karen, Teri, Laura, and Kristen.

MARIE

A human life is like a candle. It is lit when a baby is born. It reaches out perhaps at first only in the effect even a very tiny life can have on the immediate family. But with every year of growth the light grows stronger and spreads farther. Sometimes it has to struggle for brightness, but sometimes the inner light is strong and bright from the very beginning and grows with the years.

ELEANOR ROOSEVELT

Contents

Introduction

Harry S Truman once remarked that he hoped "some day someone will take time to evaluate the true role of the wife of a President, and to assess the many burdens she has to bear and the contribution she makes." He would likely be pleased by the fact that there are literally hundreds of published books detailing the First Ladies' efforts and contributions—and many of these volumes are exceptional scholarly works based on painstaking research of letters, diaries, and manuscripts, as well as carefully documented interviews with both First Ladies and their descendants.

Yet our curiosity persists. In the face of personal tragedy, public scrutiny, war, and constant love of country, we long to know what these women thought, felt, and believed. Many of their husbands prayed for strength, read the Bible, and sought divine wisdom. What about the ladies? With the pressures of living under a microscope, entertaining hundreds of people on a regular basis, and caring for their families through political highs and lows, how did they cope?

Many of the First Ladies left no memoirs, diaries, or correspondence. Thus it is not possible to have documented proof of the personal beliefs and prayers of all the talented women who have served the United States of America in the role of First Lady. Yet what endures, regardless of whether their thoughts were written down and preserved, are the stories of the First Ladies—their actions, legacies, and their children's memories. We have chosen to include in this book the stories of thirty of these remarkable women who proved to be models of steadfast faith.

The Bible speaks of the beauty of a woman coming from within. Her true bloom is seen in a gentle spirit, a choice to put all hope in God, and a desire to love and honor her husband (1 Peter 3:4–5). It is not surprising that Americans have most celebrated the First Ladies who were compassionate, generous, caring, and strongly supportive of their husbands' efforts. Such attributes reveal a heart shaped by God.

Martha Dandridge Custis Washington

1731-1802

Her case is more to be envied than pitied, for if we mortals can distinguish between those who are deserving of Grace & who are not, I am confident she enjoys that Bliss prepar'd only for the Good & virtuous. Let these considerations, My dear Mother have their due weight with you, & comfort yourself with reflecting that she now enjoys in substance what we in this world enjoy in imagination, & that there is no real Happiness on this side of the Grave. I must allow that to sustain a Shock of this kind requires more Philosophy than we in general are possest [*sic*] of, my Nature could not bear the Shock, but sunk under the load of oppression, and hindered me from administering any consolation to my dear & nearest relation; this Letter is the first thing I have done since I receiv'd the melancholy News. . . . I will no longer detain you on a subject which is painful to us both, but conclude with beging [*sic*] you to remember you are a Christian & that we ought to submit with Patience to the divine Will.

IN A LETTER FROM MARTHA'S SON, JOHN PARKE CUSTIS,
ON RECEIVING WORD OF THE DEATH OF HIS SISTER PATSY
NEW YORK, JULY 5, 1773

LIFE AND TIMES

Years before the White House even existed, Martha Dandridge Custis Washington became the first of the First Ladies and set an example of hospitality and determination for succeeding Presidents' wives to emulate.

Born on a plantation outside of Williamsburg, Virginia, on June 2, 1731, Martha was the eldest daughter born to John and Frances Dandridge. Although she lacked much formal education, she learned what it takes to keep a household content and in order.

At the age of eighteen, the five-foot-tall, dark-haired Martha married Daniel Parke Custis. They had four children, two of whom died in infancy. The other two, Patsy and John, were still toddlers when Daniel Custis passed away in 1757.

Two years after her husband's death, she married again. Her husband this time was George Washington, a leader in the Revolutionary War. Over the next thirty years, she faithfully stood by him through the hardships of war, caring for him and her children.

On April 30, 1789, George Washington took his oath of office in New York City, making him the first President of the United States and making Martha the First Lady. Bravely she followed her husband into unknown territory as the American government slowly came into being. Together, she and her husband set the standard for all succeeding Presidents and First Ladies.

"I think I am more like a state prisoner than anything else, there is certain bounds set for me which I must not depart from . . ." Martha Washington said in a letter to her niece. She was not entirely convinced that the role of First Lady suited her and said, "many younger and gayer women would be extremely pleased" to be where she was, but she would "much rather be at home."

In an effort to be recognized as equals to the governments of Europe, the Washingtons entertained visitors in a formal style. Despite the stiffness of this type of official entertaining, Martha managed to put guests at ease with her warm hospitality. Abigail Adams commended her for being "one of those unassuming characters which create love and esteem" during these formal gatherings and receptions.

In 1797 the Washingtons retired from public life and surrounded themselves with family, friends, and guests at their Mount Vernon residence. They stayed busy raising their two grandchildren, Eleanor and George.

Two years later George died. To ensure their privacy would be preserved, Martha burned the letters they had written. On May 22, 1802, Martha died, taken by a "severe fever." The two of them are buried at Mount Vernon.

I am still determined to be cheerful and happy,

in whatever situation I may be;

for I have also learned from experience

that the greater part of our happiness or misery

depends upon our dispositions,

and not upon our circumstances.

MARTHA WASHINGTON

INTERESTING FACTS

Martha had the unfortunate experience of outliving all four of her children. Her longest living child, John, whom the President and his wife called Jack, passed away in 1781. Martha lived another twenty-one years, comforted by Jack's two children and her husband.

Martha was a dedicated wife, accompanying her husband even to Valley Forge. She was constantly tending to her husband as well as to the many soldiers there, as evidenced by the journal entry of another military wife who was also staying in Valley Forge:

> I never in my life knew a woman so busy from early morning until late at night as was Lady Washington, providing comforts for the sick soldiers. Everyday, excepting Sunday, the wives of the officers in camp, and sometimes other women, were invited . . . to assist her in knitting socks, patching garments, and make shirts for the poor soldiers, when materials could be procured. Every fair day she might be seen, with basket in hand, and with a single attendant.

Martha went to church all of her life and apparently was a strong believer in prayer, an activity that began during her childhood. It is said that she regularly closed her door for an hour each morning as she spent time with the Lord and read her Bible. It is believed that her daughter-in-law, Nelly, read to Martha in her old age, generally from the Psalms, before Martha went to bed.

Martha was the first woman both to be portrayed on U.S. paper money (1886) and to appear on a postage stamp (1902).

When the Washingtons retired from the presidency, it seems that Martha's active lifestyle was hardly altered. "I am fairly settled down to the pleasant duties of a Virginia housewife. Steady as a clock, busy as a bee, and cheerful as a cricket."

When Martha died, one newspaper reported: "To those amiable and Christian virtues which adorn the female character, she added the dignity of manners, superiority of understanding, a mind intelligent and elevated. The silence of respectful grief is our best eulogy."

Abigail Smith Adams

1744-1818

The race is not to the swift, nor the battle to the strong, but the God of Israel is he that giveth strength and power unto his people. Trust in him at all times, ye people pour out your hearts before him. God is a refuge for us.

ABIGAIL, IN A LETTER TO JOHN ADAMS, JUNE 18, 1775

When will Mankind be convinced that true Religion is from the Heart, between Man and his creator, and not the imposition of Man or creeds and tests? [I am] assured that those who fear God and work righteousness shall be accepted of him, and that I presume of what ever sect or persuasion.

WRITING TO HER DAUGHTER-IN-LAW, LOUISA, JANUARY 3, 1818

LIFE AND TIMES

The descendant of a distinguished family, Abigail Smith was born in 1744 at Weymouth, Massachusetts. Abigail's mother was related to the prestigious Quincy family, and her father and other relatives were not only ministers but leaders in society.

Though not formally educated, this environment encouraged Abigail's love for both reading and learning in general.

Her ardor and diligence caught the attention of young John Adams, who graduated from Harvard and was at the time beginning his career in law. Their mutual passion for learning and reading led to a deep respect and a marriage that would last for more than half a century.

After John and Abigail were married in 1764, they lived in Boston. Abigail bore John three sons and two daughters in ten years. She did much of the child raising herself and also managed the farm and household alone, as John was often traveling as a circuit judge. He then served as a delegate to both Continental Congresses and later as an elected officer. John served in various posts in Europe between 1779 and 1788. Abigail and the children joined him in 1784 and lived in France and later Great Britain until their return to Massachusetts.

Learning is not attained by chance. It must be sought for with ardor and attended to with diligence.

ABIGAIL ADAMS

During their long separations, Abigail and John wrote many letters to each other. These letters depict a strong woman who was self-sufficient and extremely devoted to her family and country. The many letters also demonstrate the love Abigail felt for her "dearest" friend, as well as the great loneliness she felt when her husband was away.

John became Vice President in 1789. Abigail utilized her many years of experience acquired abroad to aid Mrs. Washington with various social events and formal entertaining. When John became President in 1797, the Adamses moved to Philadelphia, the early capital of the United States. Abigail continued a formal pattern of entertaining, even when the couple moved to the still unfinished presidential residence in Washington, D.C., in November 1800. The Adamses became the first presidential couple to call the White House home. Though the resources in the new house were sparse and Abigail often felt less than favorable toward the country's new capital (it was considered wilderness at that time) and unfinished house, she still hosted dinners and receptions and oversaw the decorating and completion of the White House.

In 1801 Abigail and John retired to Quincy and finally enjoyed the companionship they had missed during the many years of travel and public life. Abigail died in 1818 and was buried in the United First Parish Church.

I long to hear that you have declared an independancy—and by the way in the new Code of Laws which I suppose it will be necessary for you to make I desire you would Remember the Ladies, and be more generous and favourable to them than your ancestors. Do not put such unlimited power into the hands of the Husbands. Remember all Men would be tyrants if they could. If perticuliar care and attention is not paid to the Ladies we are determined to foment a Rebelion, and will not hold ourselves bound by any Laws in which we have no voice, or Representation.

ABIGAIL, IN A LETTER TO JOHN, MARCH 31, 1776

INTERESTING FACTS

Abigail did not relish political life. As she once told Thomas Jefferson, she preferred her farm to "the court of St. James, where I seldom meet with characters so inoffensive as my hens and chickens, or minds so well improved as my garden." She said, "I really believe they [the British] are more afraid of the Americans' prayers than their Swords." Some called her Mrs. President—in tribute to her outspoken opinions.

Abigail's father was a liberal Congregationalist and often traded pulpits with a fellow preacher, Ebenezer Gay, an Arminian who did not preach the doctrines of predestination, original sin, or the full divinity of Christ. Gay's emphasis was instead on the importance of reason and morality in religious life. Abigail's confession of her faith, which led to her membership in the Weymouth church on June 24, 1759, demonstrated Gay's influence on her beliefs.

Abigail was a devoted Christian. During the wars of her day, she fasted and prayed, cared for the sick and injured, and even took an early stand against slavery. Abigail enrolled one of her two Black servants in a school nearby. When people became angry about this, she responded:

> The boy is a freeman as much as any of the young men, and merely because his face is black, is he to be denied instruction, how is he to be qualified to procure a livelihood? Is this the Christian principle of doing to others as we would have others to do us? . . . I have not thought it any disgrace to my self to take him into my parlour and teach him both to read and write. . . . I hope we shall all go to Heaven together.

Dolley Payne Todd Madison

1768-1849

My dear, do not trouble yourself about it; there is nothing in this world worth caring for. Yes, believe me, I, who have lived so long, repeat to you, there is nothing in this world here below worth caring for.

DOLLEY MADISON'S WORDS SPOKEN TO AN ANXIOUS NIECE SHORTLY BEFORE MRS. MADISON'S DEATH IN JULY 1849, AS WRITTEN IN HER *MEMOIRS*

The grass withers and the flowers fall,
because the breath of the LORD blows on them.
Surely the people are grass.
The grass withers and the flowers fall,
but the word of our God stands forever.

ISAIAH 40:7–8

LIFE AND TIMES

Dolley Madison was simply the most influential woman of her day. Loved in the important social circles of America, she was known for her dress and her social skills and for helping shape the notion of the First Lady.

Born into a solemn Quaker community to John and Mary Payne, Dorothea (nicknamed Dolley) was raised with the strictest of disciplines. She came from a family that believed in hard work, plain clothes, and little humor. But Dolley was known for her open and happy disposition, which attracted much attention in the staid community of Philadelphia. She had very pale skin, piercing blue eyes, and dark, curly hair. She married a young lawyer in the city, but he died in just three years, leaving her and her two-year-old son, Payne Todd, to find their own way. She was only twenty-five years old.

[J] was beaten by Mr. and Mrs. Madison. J might have had a better chance had J faced Mr. Madison alone.

CANDIDATE CHARLES PINCKNEY,
AFTER LOSING THE ELECTION TO MADISON

James Madison was very different from Dolley. When they met, he was a lifelong bachelor, in his mid-forties, and an Episcopalian who liked his social life. The differences between the two must have been startling to Dolley's family, but the couple developed a relationship that was acknowledged by all as happy and fulfilling. They married in 1794. The marriage to a non-Quaker meant that Dolley was automatically dismissed from the Society of Friends. After her marriage Dolley discarded the somber Quaker dress and became known for her fine fashion, essentially becoming the woman who set the styles for the finer social circles of Philadelphia and Washington. Her home was the center of society during her husband's eight years as Thomas Jefferson's Secretary of State, and the President often asked her to receive guests, normally the role of the First Lady. When James Madison was elected President in 1809, Dolley began the tradition of the inaugural ball—a tradition that lives on today.

Dolley was admired not merely for her social grace but for the important role she played in her husband's presidency. In difficult circumstances she provided wisdom and tact, and her gracious warmth diffused the anger of many upset statesmen. When the British army sacked the White House during the War of 1812, she was forced to flee the city, but she insisted on returning, and, finding the President's home in ruins, she hosted government events and entertainments as usual from the Octagon house and later a place called The Seven Buildings, stating that seeing such activities would be a great encouragement to the people of the United States. Because of her bravery and can-do spirit, the nation embraced her. And, as a person who loved new ideas, Dolley went down in history as the first occupant of the White House to serve ice cream!

After leaving office, the Madisons turned their estate over to Dolley's only child, Todd Payne. He proceeded to lose all his parents' money as well as his own, so that when her husband died, Dolley was nearly penniless. She moved from her husband's plantation back to Washington, where friends assisted her until her death in 1849. At her funeral Dolley was hailed as one of America's most renowned patriots—one of the first great American women to be recognized for her wisdom, courage, and love of country.

INTERESTING FACTS

In 1795 President Washington said Dolley Madison was the "sprightliest" dancing partner he had ever had.

Perhaps Dolley is best known for her role during the War of 1812 in saving some of the most precious historical artifacts the young country had, including trunks of historical documents and a portrait of George Washington. She had to be urged to leave the capital because she did not want to abandon her post. Before she had grabbed her pet macaw and left the city in a carriage, the smoke from the British cannons was visible.

The Madisons attended the Episcopal church, and Dolley was often seen wearing a large cross. She was a regular attender at the "Sabbaths in the Speaker's Chair," which were interdenominational religious services held in Congress.

Dolley Madison was the first President's wife to be in charge of a true social cause. The Washington City Orphans' Asylum was first planned in October 1815 when Dolley donated twenty dollars and a cow and coordinated the first meeting to raise more funds and resources. She sewed clothes and helped other women to sew as well, while making friends with all classes of women and children. The children's home was built one block from the White House.

Without a struggle or apparent pain, . . . at peace with her maker, and with all the world and it with her.

DOLLEY MADISON'S NEPHEW, DESCRIBING HER DEATH,
JULY 12, 1849

Dolley was said to treat everyone warmly, whether a maid or a person of royalty. She was known for her giving spirit and cheerful perspective. When she was in need late in life, there was a great outpouring of love from those she had loved for so many years. Though her son had driven her to financial ruin, Dolley received cash gifts from friends and had her pantry stocked by those who cared about her. She continued to give of herself to causes and charities to better the lives of others, even when her own situation was rather bleak.

Elizabeth Kortright Monroe

1768-1830

She did the honors of the White House with perfect simplicity, nothing disturbed the composure of her manner.

Her manner is very gracious, and she is a regal looking lady.

GUESTS OF THE WHITE HOUSE DURING ELIZABETH MONROE'S
TERM OF SERVICE AS FIRST LADY

If you accept my words
*   and store up my commands within you,*
turning your ear to wisdom
*   and applying your heart to understanding,*
and if you call out for insight
*   and cry aloud for understanding,*
and if you look for it as for silver
*   and search for it as for hidden treasure,*
then you will understand the fear of the LORD
*   and find the knowledge of God.*
For the LORD gives wisdom,
*   and from his mouth come knowledge and understanding.*

He holds victory in store for the upright,
  he is a shield to those whose walk is blameless,
for he guards the course of the just
  and protects the way of his faithful ones.

PROVERBS 2:1–8

LIFE AND TIMES

Elizabeth Monroe is one of the most intriguing of all First Ladies. She was born in New York City in 1768. Apparently her father was a pirate who had made a fortune serving the King of England, only to lose much of it during the Revolutionary War when he refused to join the cause of the Colonials. Thus it might seem odd that Elizabeth would become one of America's most vocal patriots.

James Monroe fell in love with the beautiful young girl, and they were married when she was just seventeen years old. The couple moved to Fredericksburg, where her husband continued his law practice. But soon his political career took off, and the couple moved several times. Appointed by President Washington as the United States Minister to France, the couple, now with two children, moved to Paris during the French Revolution.

During the next two decades, the Monroes moved between Virginia and Europe, with James serving his country in various governmental roles and Elizabeth gaining a reputation as a fine hostess, a courageous woman, and a foreigner with a bit of mystery to her personality. In 1811 Monroe was asked to become Secretary of State for James Madison, and the Monroes moved from their Oak Hill plantation in Virginia to Washington D.C. Something about the city didn't fit Elizabeth well, and she began to have health problems.

When Monroe became President of the United States, Elizabeth's health problems often kept her from calling on

24

visiting dignitaries, something that was seen as a social faux pas. The wives of other governmental figures were often critical of her style, particularly when she began to reshape the customs of the White House into a more formal style, similar to that of the courts of Europe.

When her daughter Maria married, Elizabeth chose to have a small, private ceremony at the White House, breaking tradition from the extravagant, large-scale affairs that were the established style of Washington. People began sniping at Elizabeth, and she withdrew more and more, only appearing at important annual events.

Attempting to protect his wife, James refused to listen to the criticism and challenged those who spoke against her. After his term in office was over, the couple retired to their plantation. When Elizabeth died in 1830, James burned all their letters and the papers they had shared so that no one could explore their life and expose her memory to criticism. She remains one of the most mysterious and courtly First Ladies.

INTERESTING FACTS

Because James made a point of destroying all correspondence between Elizabeth and himself, there is little in the way of written history to know more fully Elizabeth's personal beliefs. She was a member of the Episcopal Church and did attend on a regular basis. She was also faithful in tithing, but beyond that information, there is no written record of her life as a woman of prayer.

We do know that she was brave. That much is recorded through a famous story that is definitely an important part of the Monroe legacy. In 1794 the Monroes were living in France when James was the American minister to France. This was a tenuous time in France—in the week before the minister arrived in Paris, the famed Robespierre had been executed. Madame de Lafayette was being held in prison and expected to face the guillotine at any time. The Monroes endeavored to save her. Here James writes of the plan he conceived and Elizabeth carried out:

> As soon as one [carriage] could be procured & equipped for me, Mrs. Monroe drove in it to her prison door, and demanded an interview with Mdme. La Fayette. All eyes were fixed on the carriage & the inquiry general, to whom it belonged. To the American minister was the answer. Mdme. La Fayette was overwhelmed by the occurrence. She ran out precipitately and frantic to the iron railing of her prison gate, to greet her unknown friend who viewed her with the utmost kindness and affection. All the spectators were affected by the scene, an account of which spread thro' Paris, & by which I have no doubt, had a happy effect in promoting her discharge, which followed soon after.

This vaulted the Monroes to fame in France, and Elizabeth became known across Europe as *la belle Américaine*.

Despite the fact that people called her aloof and even spoofed her as royalty, Elizabeth was also attacked for her allowance for certain informalities when it came to allowing all members of a very class-conscious society to mingle at Wednesday night receptions.

Elizabeth was a handsome woman. Here is one description from a guest at a party on New Year's Day, 1825: "Her dress was superb black velvet; neck and arms bare and beautifully formed; her hair in puffs and dressed high on the head and ornamented with white ostrich plumes; around her neck an elegant pearl necklace. Though no longer young, she is still a very handsome woman."

Though she was popular in France, in America Elizabeth made people angry with the way she entertained and received visitors. She was commonly called Queen Elizabeth while she lived in the White House, truly a rude jeer if ever there was one, given the fairly recent war the United States had fought with the British and the general feelings still simmering toward the mother country. And yet the social customs she developed, whether her contemporaries approved or not, were necessary and helped give dimension to the designated role of future First Ladies—and what was implemented as protocol by Elizabeth Monroe is still in practice today.

One interesting note regarding Elizabeth Monroe was the relationship she maintained with a woman quite different from herself. It is said that Elizabeth and Rachel Jackson, wife of Andrew Jackson, had a warm correspondence through their husbands, following their meeting at an event in Washington. The regal Elizabeth Monroe befriended Rachel Jackson, a portly, out-of-her-element wife who was no doubt made miserable by having to be at that social gathering. A four-year correspondence followed and did not end until Rachel died.

Louisa Catherine Johnson Adams

1775-1852

Knowing how contrary it is to my husband's principles to assist any individual of his family, I again repeat that I am shocked at the necessity of the step I am now taking; but my religion sanctions it, and I prefer my duty to God, to my duty to men.

A LETTER FROM LOUISA TO PRESIDENT JAMES MONROE,
SEEKING A GOVERNMENT APPOINTMENT FOR HER SISTER'S HUSBAND,
WHOM LOUISA'S HUSBAND, THEN SECRETARY OF STATE,
HAD REFUSED TO HELP

LIFE AND TIMES

Louisa Catherine Johnson was born in 1775 to an English mother, Catherine Nuth, and an American father, Joshua

Johnson. Unlike most presidential wives who were born and raised in America, she spent her youth in London. Some believe Louisa's cultural experiences made her haughty; whatever the case, John Quincy Adams began courting Louisa in London in 1794. The two finally married in 1797 and settled in Berlin, where John served as a diplomat. At court Louisa's ladylike manners and English sensibilities made her a perfect diplomat's wife.

When John and Louisa moved to the United States in 1801, Louisa found the New England farm community a strange new environment. With this move the couple began several years of living between homes in Quincy, Massachusetts; Boston; and Washington, D.C. When the Adamses finally made a permanent home in Washington, Louisa at last began to feel at home.

This home did not last long, however. Leaving their two older sons in America, the family moved to Russia, where John served as foreign minister. Despite enjoying the court of the Tsar, Louisa had to confront cold winters, limited funds, and continuous poor health. She was greatly saddened by the loss of a baby daughter in 1812. Two years later John was called to Ghent for peace negotiations to help end the war with Britain. From there he sent word to Louisa to dispose of their property in St. Petersburg and join him in Europe.

Louisa's journey to join her husband in Paris was frightening, and she had only a few staff members to help her. She and her son traveled by coach across the continent, surviving the bitterly cold winter weather and the roving bands of stragglers and highwaymen. After forty days they arrived in Paris. Later John would be appointed to serve in London, and the family would remain there for two years.

In 1817, when John was appointed Secretary of State, the family moved back to Washington, D.C. Louisa opened her home to the growing number of diplomats and became known as a generous hostess whose theater parties and good music were well known. John was elected President in 1825, but the bitter political debate surrounding the election made entertaining less enjoyable for Louisa. Though she still hosted her weekly "drawing rooms," depression and poor health led her to favor quiet evenings at home where she read, composed music and poetry, and played the harp. John lost his bid for reelection, but Louisa managed to entertain until the end, hosting an elegant last reception that reflected her still vibrant hospitality.

John and Louisa returned to Massachusetts for a short time but went back to Washington when John began seventeen years of service in the House of Representatives. One year after celebrating their fiftieth wedding anniversary, John died suddenly at the capitol. Louisa died four years later and is now buried next to John at the family church in Quincy.

They tell me that it was the act of the Almighty, but oh, can anything compensate for the agony of this last parting on earth, after fifty years of union, without even the privilege of indulging the feelings which all hold sacred at such moments. My senses almost gave way, and it seemed to me as if I had become callous to suffering, while my heart seemed breaking.

IN A LETTER FROM LOUISA TO HER SISTER HERRIET,
AFTER JOHN QUINCY ADAMS DIED

INTERESTING FACTS

For what appears to be the vast majority of their years of marriage, John and Louisa were not a close couple. They spent long periods of time apart, even on different continents, and even when they were under the same roof, particularly in the White House, the two still tended to operate in isolation. While First Lady, Louisa struggled with depression. In 1840 she began writing *Adventures of a Nobody*, a story of her struggles and personal regrets. To help herself feel better, and to cope with her feelings, she ate pounds and pounds of chocolates, sketched, cultivated silkworms, and read books. She did not appear to have close friends, and her husband withdrew into his own bitter world following the election.

Along with an estimated twelve pregnancies, which included seven miscarriages and one stillbirth, Mrs. Adams had physical ailments. Her three children (a fourth died in infancy) were precious to her, and the suicide of their oldest son, George—Washington's namesake—when he was just twenty-seven in 1828 was very difficult. It was also the event that brought Louisa and John Quincy closer together, at last.

*There is something in this great
unsocial house [the White House]
which depresses my spirits beyond expression
and makes it impossible for me to feel at home
or to fancy that I have a home any where.*

GEORGE ADAMS, IN A LETTER TO LOUISA

During Andrew Jackson's presidency, Louisa developed some sympathy for oppressed African Americans. She heard of a slave family that was being divided up and sold, and she contributed fifty dollars to help free them. She also bought the title to a slave woman who worked as a cook and later set the woman free. Of that experience, she wrote that she was "almost as glad as if I was buying my own freedom."

Rachel Donelson Robards Jackson

1767-1828

My judg will know how many prayers have I oferd up.

RACHEL'S TESTIMONY TO PRAYING FOR HER ENEMIES
PRIOR TO THE ELECTION OF 1824

Oh for Zion! I am not at rest, nor can I be, in this heathen land.

IN A LETTER FROM RACHEL TO HER HUSBAND,
WHILE HE SERVED AS GOVERNOR OF FLORIDA

LIFE AND TIMES

Born on the American frontier in 1767, Rachel Donelson grew up traveling with her family through the wilds of Kentucky, Tennessee, and what is now West Virginia. Other than learning how to read the Bible and the bare essentials of spelling, she was uneducated, as were most women of the frontier. Rachel married the son of a Kentucky scion when she was only seventeen, but Lewis Robards's insane jealousy caused her to leave him. They separated, and Rachel was told her husband was filing for divorce. A few years later, she met and married Andrew Jackson, a rough-hewn former soldier with a passion for politics and justice. He was a successful lawyer, but as he became more involved with politics, it was clear his strong opinions could lead to divisiveness.

After two years in a very happy marriage, the couple learned that Rachel's first husband had never in fact completed the divorce proceedings. Instead, he charged Rachel with adultery. The situation took nearly two years to resolve, and in 1794 Rachel and Andrew remarried. She had made an honest mistake, but Jackson's political enemies were always quick to whisper of adultery and bigamy.

In the bitter election of 1828, Andrew Jackson won a narrow victory over the incumbent President John Quincy Adams. During the election, some supporters of Adams had dredged up the old accusations against Rachel. One handbill, which is said to have circulated at this time, said: "Ought a convicted adulteress and her paramour husband to be placed in the highest offices of this free and christian land?" The fiery Jackson was quick to defend any slight against his wife, but he was only one man opposing an entire army of press, politicians, and other candidates.

Although her husband made every effort to shield her from these attacks, it is believed she found either a piece of literature in town or overheard a conversation and was made aware of the new attacks on her character. Heartbroken, she became sick and died on Christmas Eve, just weeks after the election and three months before her husband would take office. She was buried in the gown she had purchased for Andrew's inauguration, with the ceremony and burial taking place at the Hermitage. After her death, one of Rachel's nieces, Emily Donelson, served in the role as White House hostess, and then later the role fell to Andrew Jackson's daughter-in-law, Sarah Yorke Jackson.

At Rachel's graveside Andrew was overheard speaking these words to his wife: "In the presence of this dear saint I can and do forgive all my enemies. But those vile wretches who have slandered her must look to God for mercy."

A being so gentle and so virtuous slander might wound, but could not dishonor.

LINES FROM RACHEL'S EPITAPH

INTERESTING FACTS

Rachel did not hide the fact that she never wanted to be in the White House. With friends she often paraphrased Psalm 84:10: "I'd rather be a doorkeeper in the house of God, than to dwell in *that palace in Washington.*"

Rachel was extremely religious. She always traveled with her Bible, and, besides being in touch with friends and family, attending church was her only activity. A brick Presbyterian church was constructed near their home in Tennessee, with Andrew Jackson making the largest contribution to its construction.

Mrs. Jackson was the opposite of her husband—gentle, kind, and a lover of strangers. She opened up their home to everyone; she was "Aunt Rachel" to many in the neighborhood. Since she and Andrew never had children of their own, they welcomed the visits of her relatives' children. In 1809 they adopted their nephew Andrew Jackson Jr., and they raised several other children.

Rachel was eulogized by her pastor, Rev. William Hume: "While we cordially sympathize with the President of the United States in the irreparable loss he sustained in the death of his amiable lady, whom he deemed so worthy, as he said, of our tears; we cannot doubt but that she now dwells in the mansions of glory in company with the ransomed of the Lord."

What, what has been done in one week!

Great order was observed; the doors kept shut;

the gambling houses demolished;

fiddling and dancing not heard any more

on the Lord's day; cursing not to be heard.

RACHEL, AFTER SUCCESSFULLY CAJOLING HER HUSBAND INTO ISSUING
A SABBATARIAN ORDER WHILE HE WAS GOVERNOR OF FLORIDA

Hannah Hoes Van Buren

1783-1819

She was a sincere Christian, a dutiful child, tender mother, affectionate wife. Precious shall be the memory of her virtues.

EPITAPH OF HANNAH VAN BUREN

LIFE AND TIMES

Born in 1783 and raised in the Dutch village of Kinderhook, New York, Hannah Hoes grew up not far from her cousin Martin Van Buren. The two were sweethearts for years, but Martin's law practice was slow to succeed, so they put off marriage until they were both nearly twenty-four years old—a considerable delay in that day. Little can be gleaned of Hannah's life from her husband's papers. He didn't even use her name when writing his autobiography late in life. But other family members referred to her as loving, gentle, and modest to the point of timidity. She was very involved with the Dutch Reformed Church and considered membership in the church a vital part of her life.

The couple was apparently quite content with their rather limited world, and they had several sons while living in Kinderhook. But in 1816 the family moved to Albany, where Martin's business grew, and he became involved in state politics. Martin's law partner, the three clerks they had apprenticing with them, as well as various relatives from upstate New York, all lived in the Van Buren home. Letters from the time reveal Hannah as a busy and sociable mother, very committed to her Christian faith, but someone who began having health problems while still relatively young.

Hannah became sick with tuberculosis, and she passed away on February 5, 1819, two years after the birth of the couple's fifth son. She was just thirty-five years old. At that point Martin announced he would never remarry. Though he became quite wealthy and must certainly have had women interested in him, he remained single and kept a painting of Hannah with him the rest of his life. Eighteen years after his wife's death, the longtime widower was elected President of the United States.

One interesting note about Hannah Van Buren is the influence she had on her husband's taste. She had always been a stylish woman, and when Martin moved into the White House, he found a shabby place that the widower Andrew Jackson had let fall into disrepair. Van Buren immediately took steps to refurbish it and make it an elegant home once again.

Former First Lady Dolley Madison still lived just blocks away, and Van Buren called on her to assist with the renovation. On one visit, she brought with her a niece, Angelica Singleton of South Carolina. Angelica's beauty and manners caught the attention of the President's eldest son, Abraham. The couple were married just one year into Martin's presidency, and Angelica often presided as First Lady at state dinners and presidential parties.

INTERESTING FACTS

Little is known about Hannah other than what is recorded below about her Christian virtue. When the Van Burens lived in Albany, New York, Hannah gained great favor with the Reverend John Chester by being in favor of organizing a Sunday school in Albany to "teach the unlettered waifs of the street to read." Most of the other women of the church were not interested due to the fact that it would mean inviting people from a lower level of society into the church, mingling with them, and welcoming them. Supposedly Hannah warmly supported the project.

This was during a time when Sunday school programs were a means of outreach into the community rather than programs for teaching those already attending church. This was the model for Sunday school started by Robert Raikes of Gloucester, England, in 1780 when he hired women to teach the poor and homeless how to read.

Hannah gave birth to five sons, with four of them living to adulthood. Before Hannah passed away, she called her sons to her and "committed them to the care of the Savior she loved." She instructed her husband to spend no money on a funeral and instead give the funds to the poor. A niece spoke of Hannah's "loving, gentle disposition."

Hannah was buried in Second Presbyterian Church, Albany, New York, but in 1855, her body was exhumed and reburied at the Kinderhook Cemetery, where her husband was later buried in 1862.

The obituary of Hannah Van Buren appeared in the Albany *Argus* on February 8, 1819, and is believed to have been written by her pastor, Rev. Chester. Here is part of what he wrote:

> As a daughter and a sister, wife and a mother, her loss is deeply deplored, for in all these varied relations, she was affectionate, tender and truly estimable. But the tear of

sorrow is almost dried by the reflection that she lived possessing the most engaging simplicity of manners, her heart was for the wants and sufferings of others. Her temper was uncommonly mild and sweet, her bosom was filled with benevolence and content—no love of show, no ambitious desires, no pride of ostentation ever disturbed its peace. . . . Humility was her crowning grace; she possessed it in rare degree; it took root and flourished full and flair, shedding over every act of her life its general influence. She was an ornament of the Christian faith.

Anna Tuthill Symmes Harrison

1775-1864

I hope my dear, you will always bear upon your mind that you are born to die and we know not how soon death may overtake us, it will be of little consequence if we are rightly prepared for the event.

. . . I hope you will not suffer yourself to forget your dear little brother who has left us for the world of spirits. . . . May the God of all mercies bless, protect you and keep you in the paths of virtue.

ANNA, IN A LETTER TO HER SON WILLIAM IN 1819 WHEN HE WAS A
STUDENT AT TRANSYLVANIA COLLEGE

LIFE AND TIMES

Anna Harrison never wanted her husband to run for the presidency. They had been married for more than forty years and been through a considerable amount of difficulty, so

41

she didn't like the idea of her sixty-eight-year-old husband's traveling from their home in Ohio all the way to Washington, D.C.

Mingling my tears with the sighs
of the many patriots of the land,
J pray to heaven for the enduring happiness
and prosperity of our beloved Country.

ANNA'S RESPONSE TO THE OFFICIAL DOCUMENT FROM CONGRESS,
CALLED THE RESOLUTIONS OF CONDOLENCES,
EXPRESSING GRATITUDE FOR PRESIDENT HARRISON'S
PATRIOTISM AND SERVICE

In fact, Anna Tuthill Symmes Harrison had already experienced more adventure than most people will ever know. She had grown up in cities and been sent away for a proper education to New York when she was just fourteen—later becoming the first woman with a formal education to serve as First Lady. Her mother died shortly after Anna's birth, and Anna went to live with her maternal grandparents when she was four years old. They raised her and provided for her schooling. At age nineteen, when her father set out to stake a land settlement in the wilderness area of Ohio, Anna went along—hoping to find adventure and taking her finest dresses in a trunk so she could share some culture with the families on the Western frontier.

In the summer of 1795, she met a tough young soldier by the name of William Henry Harrison. He too had come from a good family in the East, and he too had gone west in search of adventure. Anna's father didn't want his daughter marrying a man who would take her to the Wild West, so the couple were married in secret. Her father said, "He is a man who can neither bleed [as a doctor], plead [as a lawyer], nor preach, and if he could plow I should be satisfied." After struggling with her family's objections, Anna and William moved several times, often living a spartan existence in frontier forts. She learned to live with danger, few luxuries, and the possibility of losing her husband in battles with Indians.

After William won fame as a hero of the War of 1812, he left the service for a career in politics, serving as territorial delegate from Ohio and later being appointed Governor of Indiana Territory. But each move seemed to take the family farther from civilization. Eventually they built a home in Indiana Territory at Vincennes, which they called a plantation but most everyone else referred to as a fort. The couple had several children, and Anna often cared for them alone, when her husband was off on governmental business. Later they retired to the family farm in Ohio, but William was regularly called on to take leadership roles for the government.

When the Whigs nominated William for the U.S. presidency, Anna opposed it, saying she wished "my husband's friends had left him where he is, happy and contented." Instead, Harrison ran and won, then faced a cross-country journey in winter to arrive in Washington for his inauguration. Anna, tired of their travels and not wishing a return to East Coast civilization, decided not to travel with him. She said she'd go in the spring, when the weather had improved. Instead, their daughter-in-law traveled with William. During the campaign, much had been made of his age, so William decided to walk in the inaugural parade rather than ride. At a friend's suggestion, he walked without an overcoat in an attempt to prove his vigor for the job.

The day of the inauguration was chilly and wet. Harrison caught a cold, which quickly led to pneumonia, and he died just a month after taking the oath of office. By the time Anna heard, she had not even finished packing for the trip to join him. She never traveled to Washington, instead choosing to stay at their home in Ohio. She lived until the age of eighty-eight, a dignified woman who had experienced a life of adventure.

INTERESTING FACTS

A faithful Presbyterian, Mrs. Harrison was a strict Sabbath keeper, insisting it be a day of rest with no official business being conducted. Attending church was a key part of her week, and it was common practice for the Harrisons to host a church dinner, or Sunday feast as they came to be called, with as many as fifty people attending any one Sunday.

From my earliest childhood, the frivolous amusements of youth had no charms for me.

ANNA HARRISON

A visitor to the Harrisons during the 1840 campaign said, "Mrs. Harrison is one of the handsomest old ladies I ever saw, a perfect beauty, and such a *good* person."

Anna gave birth to ten children—four boys and six girls, the largest number of children borne by any First Lady. One of them, Lucy Singleton Harrison, was born on the banks of the James River during a trip to visit a relative. Anna outlived all of her children, except for her son John Scott, who was the father of the twenty-third President, Benjamin Harrison.

As she suffered through her many losses, Anna must have relied greatly on the Lord. Between 1836 and 1846, Anna buried six of her children and her husband. The Harrisons' children were

44

Elizabeth (1796–1846)
John (1798–1830)
Lucy (1800–1826)
William (1802–1838)
John Scott (1804–1878)
Benjamin (1806–1840)
Mary (1809–1842)
Carter (1811–1839)
Anna (1813–1845)
James (1818–1819)

Anna Harrison was the first wife of a President to be widowed while her husband was in office. As a presidential widow, Congress awarded Anna a twenty-five-thousand-dollar stipend, and she was also given the franking privilege, which allowed her to send mail free of charge.

Letitia Christian Tyler

1790-1842

There was no lip service in Letitia Tyler's religion. She accepted the theology of her church as unquestioningly as she accepted all of the other standards of her time. But her piety came from the heart.

Biographer Mary Whitton

The most entirely unselfish person you can imagine.

Priscilla Cooper Tyler, Letitia's daughter-in-law

In the month of September, 1842, died Letitia Christian Tyler. She had been the victim of paralysis for four years previous, but with exemplary patience, had borne its suffering. She was a wife, a mother, and a Christian, loving and confiding to her husband, gentle and affectionate to her children, kind and charitable to the needy and afflicted.

Obituary printed in the National Intelligencer

LIFE AND TIMES

The daughter of a planter and politician, Letitia was born in 1790 and grew up about twenty miles east of Richmond, Virginia. She is remembered for her gentle manner and beautiful eyes. There is only one portrait of her that remains, as well as a single engraving that was based on that painting.

Letitia and John had a rather restrained courtship—it is said that he never even kissed her hand until three weeks before the wedding! Tyler wrote that he was relieved he wasn't wealthy, since it ruled out the possibility that she was accepting him for personal gain. Instead, their union was based on love. The couple married in 1813 and produced nine children, with two dying in infancy.

Letitia Tyler was not particularly remarkable, but she certainly was a fine wife and mother. Her husband once said of her: "She was perfectly content to be seen only as a part of the existence of her beloved husband; to entertain her neighbors; to sit gently by her child's cradle, reading, knitting, or sewing." When John Tyler was elected to the Senate in 1827, he wanted his wife to be near him, but she was happier remaining at home on their Virginia plantation. In 1828–29, however, she spent one social season in Washington, when her husband was Governor of Virginia.

As Harrison's Vice President, Tyler became President following Harrison's death. By then Letitia had been confined to a wheelchair for two years. Originally, to be with his wife, John had planned to handle his vice-presidential duties from his home in Virginia. When he became President, however, Letitia moved to the White House with her husband in short order.

Though Letitia managed some of the details of First Lady, the actual hostess duties were left to her daughter-in-law, Priscilla Cooper Tyler, wife of son Robert. The only actual event that Letitia Tyler attended was the wedding of her daughter Elizabeth to William N. Walker on January 3, 1842. "Lizzie looked surpassingly lovely," said Priscilla, and "our dear mother" was "far more attractive to me . . . than any other lady in the room," greeting her guests "in her sweet, gentle, self-possessed manner."

Letitia was the first President's wife to die in the White House. Holding a damask rose, she quietly passed away on September 10, 1842, following a second stroke. She was buried in Virginia at the plantation of her birth, and her family deeply mourned her passing.

In June 1844, while he was still President, John married Julia Gardiner.

I could not hold up to you a better pattern for your imitation than is constantly presented by your dear mother. You never see her course marked with precipitation; but on the contrary, everything is brought before the tribunal of her judgment, and her actions are all founded on prudence. Follow her example, my dear daughter, and you will be . . . a great source of comfort to me.

JOHN TYLER, TO HIS DAUGHTER MARY, PRAISING HIS WIFE'S LIFE

INTERESTING FACTS

Letitia, though not formally educated, was a skilled manager of the Tyler plantation and had considerable success handling business matters while her husband worked for many years in the political arena, as a Senator, Governor, Vice President, and President.

Like so many from the area where the family's plantation was located, the Tylers struggled somewhat with the social demands of the political system, given that they were rich in land but had little extra in the way of money. Thus, in part, Letitia stayed at home during her husband's political career out of necessity. It was said that she "maintained by her active economy the pecuniary independence of her husband under his continued public employment." After John became President, Letitia worried constantly about the continuous drain on the family finances, since at this point in history, Congress insisted that the President pay all expenses out of his own pocket.

Letitia was most comfortable with her Bible, prayer book, and knitting at her side. She taught her children to read using the family Bible. Toward the end of her life, it was observed by one visitor that she was "always found seated in her large arm-chair, with a small stand by her side, which holds her Bible and prayer book—the only books she ever reads now."

Sarah Childress Polk

1803-1891

I recognize nothing in myself; I am only an atom in the hands of God.

Sarah Polk

LIFE AND TIMES

As the elder daughter of Captain Joel and Elizabeth Childress, Sarah enjoyed a lavish plantation life in Murfreesboro, Tennessee—a life that included the rare gift of education. Sarah's father insisted both she and her younger sister attend school, first in Nashville and then at the Moravians' Female Academy in Salem. This education provided Sarah with a solid foundation in history, literature, and manners, equipping her well for her future role as the wife of a President.

It also brought her into the path of James Polk. It is believed Andrew Jackson helped bring the young people together by suggesting she would be a good match for James. Sarah and James were married in 1824 on New Year's Day, shortly after James began his first year of service in the Tennessee Legislature.

From the beginning Sarah took an active role in her husband's work. She was unable to have children, so she involved herself fully in politics and placed herself at her husband's disposal. While no contemporary woman would have openly admitted to serving in a political role, Sarah accompanied her husband to Washington whenever possible and soon endeared herself and her husband to the most elite social circles. Sarah aided her husband in writing speeches, copied his correspondence, advised him, and watched over his health.

The strict moral training Sarah gained during her time with the Moravians shaped her the remainder of her life. Known as a devout Presbyterian, Sarah never attended horse races or the theater and banned dancing, card playing, and most liquor in the White House.

The greater the prosperity, the deeper the sense of gratitude to the Almighty.

SARAH POLK

When James was elected President in 1845 and they moved to the White House, Sarah gladly stepped into place beside him as the First Lady. Sarah's style of managing and entertaining was contrasted sharply with that of the former First Lady, because Sarah took no pleasure in parties or elegant gatherings. Yet she maintained important social contacts, and her skillful conversation led to wide popularity and respect.

James's term in office was draining. The stress eventually weakened his immune system, and he could not ward off fever. Only three months after retiring from the presidency, he died. Sarah lived for forty-two years after his death, always dressed in black and always living at Polk Place in Nashville.

Sarah continued to garner respect for her intelligence and friendly spirit. In fact, as the Civil War tore the country apart, Sarah refrained from supporting either side and hosted dinners for both Confederate and Union leaders.

In 1891 Sarah Polk died at the age of eighty-eight and was buried beside her husband.

INTERESTING FACTS

Sarah was considered very serious and religious, and except for her love of politics, she was the quintessential proper lady of that era. She was known to remain behind with the men to talk, rather than retire to the parlor with the ladies. It is said that Sarah was happy to debate and discuss politics, and she gained high compliments from men such as Henry Clay and Andrew Jackson for her sharp mind and quick wit. Future President Franklin Pierce once said he preferred to discuss politics with Sarah than with her husband.

Sarah was quite willing to use her wit with anyone. After once meeting an older woman who was supportive of Henry Clay during the 1844 campaign, this exchange took place: The woman told Sarah that Mrs. Clay would make an excellent First Lady because she was a good housekeeper and made excellent butter. Sarah responded with a measured look and told the woman that if James won the election, she would easily live within the salary given him and wouldn't have to make her own butter to do it.

Though she dressed in black after her husband's death, during her younger years she wore more vibrant shades of blue, red, and maroon. All of these shades suited her dark coloring, which contributed to her nickname, "Sahara Sarah."

Sarah was known for her prudence. She was given money to refurbish the White House and had gas lighting installed in 1846. Despite this expense, she was able to save half of the money allotted for redecorating. A humorous side note of history is that on the eve of the debut of the new gas lighting, the system failed! Thankfully, Sarah had placed candles in the room just in case.

Sarah believed dancing was improper, and it was she who was responsible for the ban that was not to be lifted until Caroline Harrison restored dancing to the White House in 1889. As Sarah explained:

> [Dancing] would be respectful neither to the house nor to the office. How indecorous it would seem for dancing to be going on in one apartment, while in another we were conversing with dignitaries of the republic or ministers of the gospel. This unseemly juxtaposition would be likely to occur at any time, were such amusements permitted.

She did decide to have "Hail to the Chief" played whenever her husband entered the room at social functions, as he was not tall and the tune made people more aware of his arrival on the scene. She was the first to call for the tune's routine use, although Julia Tyler was the first person to suggest it be used to announce the President's arrival.

In the spring of 1845, not long after her husband's inauguration, Sarah visited Dolley Madison and asked for advice and suggestions on how she ought to entertain. That she was humble enough to defer to Dolley says much about Sarah's nature, and yet Dolley told her that she would have to find her own way, ultimately, since times change and entertaining must change to fit the style of the person in the White House. Sarah ended up finding a middle ground and carried off her duties very well—no doubt in part because of the encouragement of Dolley Madison.

Mrs. Polk was a Sabbatarian and made it her duty to keep official business conducted on Sunday to a minimum, if not eliminate it altogether. She was famous for inviting whoever was speaking with her husband to church when it came time to leave the White House for service. As a result, people began to avoid the White House on Sundays, which was just what Sarah wanted.

One Sunday a politician, who was well aware of Mrs. Polk's reputation for inviting visitors to church, decided to tease her. When she came into the room to fetch her husband for services, she was particularly eager as there was to be a new preacher. The visitor said cheerfully, "Then I would like to go with you, madam, for I have played cards with him many a time!"

Abigail Powers Fillmore

1798-1853

For twenty-seven years, my entire married life, I was always greeted with a happy smile.

MILLARD FILLMORE

For to a person who is good in His sight He has given wisdom and knowledge and joy.

ECCLESIASTES 2:26 NASB

LIFE AND TIMES

Born in Saratoga County, New York, in 1798, Abigail Powers was the daughter of a prominent Baptist minister who died not long after her birth. Her mother, taking a huge risk, decided the small amount of money she had left would go further in a wilderness area, so she moved herself and her two children to the frontier. Using her late husband's extensive library, she schooled her children at home—giving them a much better education than was usually found in the American West.

At sixteen Abigail began to teach at a country school. She met her future husband when he was her student for a period of several months at New Hope Academy. Though she started teaching at a young age, she never stopped reading and learning to better educate herself. Referring to her as his "inspiration," Millard Fillmore went on to study law and started his own law firm. It proved to be a struggle, and though the couple wanted to marry, they had to wait. When they finally were wed, Abigail was nearly twenty-eight, older than was normal for the time. After the birth of their first child, Abigail returned to teaching, thereby becoming the first of the First Ladies to hold a job after marriage.

When success finally came for the Fillmores, they bought a large house in Buffalo. It was there that Abigail learned the polite manners of society, as her husband was elected first to Congress, then to a New York State office. Poor health, in particular a badly broken ankle, and her own desire to focus on reading and music caused Abigail to withdraw from some public functions, but she became known for her flower garden and her commitment to helping others learn to read.

In 1849 Millard Fillmore was elected Vice President of the United States under Zachary Taylor, and the family moved to Washington. Less than a year and a half later, the President died, and the Fillmores moved into the White House.

It was a difficult time for the country, with pitched battles over slavery and rumors of secession. The society parties became more subdued, and Abigail often withdrew to focus on reading or music in private. Most difficult for her were the Friday night "levees," in which she was asked to stand on her bad ankle for two hours, greeting guests and welcoming dignitaries. She was known to talk books with guests, and one of the great joys of her life occurred in 1851, when Congress appropriated money for a White House library. Abigail took charge of that project, spending many hours selecting and arranging the books in the Oval Office, which at the time housed her piano, guitar, and harp. During this time, people on all sides of the secession debate grew to appreciate the First Lady's commitment to reading and teaching.

Though she was recognized as a gracious hostess, Abigail continued to struggle with health problems and often asked her daughter Abby to stand in for her at routine social functions. When Franklin Pierce won the election of 1852, Abigail oversaw the inaugural ceremonies. Much of it took place outside, and a cold northeast wind blew snow over the crowd. On returning to the Willard Hotel where she was staying, Abigail said she had a chill. The chill turned into a cold, which quickly developed into pneumonia. She died there on March 30, 1853. Out of respect for her, both the House and Senate adjourned and all public offices were closed. Abigail Powers Fillmore was buried near her home in Buffalo.

INTERESTING FACTS

Abigail was a country schoolteacher and only nineteen when Millard Fillmore appeared in her classroom in the winter of 1818. Noting the big farm boy, Abigail asked him to come to her desk and said, "I don't think I have your name." He told her his name and appeared eager to learn. He was eighteen. The President would later sum up their relationship in those early years with these words: "I pursued much of my study with, and perhaps was unconsciously stimulated by, the companionship of a young lady whom I afterward married."

During their courtship, Millard and Abigail had little money to travel to see one another, and so for three years they courted by mail. Abigail remained in Sempronius, New York, while Millard traveled to Buffalo, 150 miles away, to continue his law studies.

Once Mrs. Fillmore went to the racetrack with her daughter and bet a pair of gloves on the outcome. She lost!

Abigail is perhaps best known for starting the White House library. When she first came to that home, she was appalled by the fact that there wasn't a Bible or a dictionary to be found. Then her husband managed to get two thousand dollars for her to start a library in the Oval Office. She picked out the volumes that would grow into the library now present. Her other contributions included convincing the President to end the practice of flogging in the Navy. She also tried to convince him to veto the Fugitive Slave Bill but was not successful.

As First Lady, Abigail used her position to help those who asked, including her brother, David Powers, who needed a job. She was instrumental in developing a following from among her friends for a young dressmaker. The public's image of the First Lady was warm—her photo was requested many times for the newspaper.

Abigail did a great service for a forgotten writer, Mrs. S. Helen De Kroyft. Helen had been blind for seven years, and she had had to give up her writing. On one occasion she was brought to the White House to visit Abigail, who became friends with the writer and eventually introduced her to a doctor, recently arrived from London. The result of this encounter was shared with Abigail in this letter:

Dear Mrs. Fillmore,

I shall see again. . . . Never, never shall I look on the flowers, or the white snow of winter, or the blue sky, but I shall remember to whom I owe it all. . . . You have made my heart glad, and now at last, you have turned my dark steps toward the light. . . . I thank you, I bless you, I love you, and all the time I shall pray for you.

YOUR MOST HUMBLE, MOST DEVOTED FRIEND,
S. HELEN DE KROYFT

Jane Means Appleton Pierce

1806-1863

Other refuge have I none.

THE LAST WORDS OF FIRST LADY JANE PIERCE

Many a time, have I gone [to church] from respect to her,
when, if left to my own choice, I should have remained
in the house.

SECRETARY TO PRESIDENT PIERCE

LIFE AND TIMES

Jane Pierce was a quiet, retiring woman who never sought
attention nor wanted a public role. It seemed that all the
events of her life pushed her toward society but at the same
time brought her sorrow.

She was known as a sensitive and shy girl with a sweet
personality and weak constitution. Her father, a Congregational minister and former president of Bowdoin College,

was well known for his hospitality, but his family found his public role difficult. He died when Jane was a teen, and she moved with her mother to Amherst, New Hampshire. There she met a lawyer by the name of Franklin Pierce, who happened to be a Bowdoin graduate and had stopped to visit Jane's mother. The two young people fell in love and were married after an extremely long courtship. Jane's mother opposed the marriage, and Jane wasn't sure she wanted to link her life to someone with political aspirations and the social responsibilities entailed by such a union.

Franklin's star was indeed on the rise. He served in several government posts and was eventually elected to the United States Senate. The couple finally married (when Jane was twenty-eight and considered a bit of a spinster), and they had a son just a year later. Tragically, the boy died days after his birth, sending Jane into a deep depression. A year later another son died of typhus. Franklin, who was devoted to his wife, decided to retire while at the height of his career.

In 1846 he joined the United States Army to serve during the war with Mexico. He earned the rank of brigadier, gained fame as a war hero, then returned to his quiet life in New Hampshire with Jane and their little son, Benjamin. In 1852 the Democratic Party made Franklin Pierce their candidate for President. Jane fainted when she read the news, and Franklin took his wife on an extended vacation to try to convince her of the potential good that could come if he were elected. But just weeks after his victory, on January 6, 1853, as the family was traveling home by train, their car derailed and Benjamin was killed. He was eleven.

All of America shared the grief of the President-elect and his wife. There was no inaugural ball, as had become the tradition, and Jane didn't even attend the inauguration. The previous First Lady, Abigail Fillmore, filled in for her at the White House functions. It was a gloomy four-year term, made worse by Mrs. Fillmore's sudden death in March 1853, followed by the death of Vice President Rufus King a month later.

Jane Pierce forced herself to meet the social obligations of her role, but she never enjoyed it. She would lock herself in her upstairs bedroom for hours at a time and eventually was given the nickname "The Shadow of the White House."

Surrounded by a small circle of close friends from New Hampshire, Jane turned to her Christian faith. She was known to spend hours in prayer, reading her Bible, and being quietly alone in her room. She wrote letters to her precious boys and mourned for them. Those in government and society respected her grief and her privacy and, recognizing that her physical health was fragile, did not put great demands on her.

After four years of sadness and seeing the country begin to split over the issue of slavery, Franklin Pierce knew he'd had enough. Determined to care for his wife, he refused to run for reelection, instead taking Jane on a long trip abroad in search of alternative health remedies. It's said that Jane carried her son Benjamin's Bible with her for the entire journey. Apparently their quest for peace abroad was unsuccessful, for the couple moved back to their home in New Hampshire so that Jane could be near family and friends. She died just a few years later and was buried in the family plot next to her beloved children.

INTERESTING FACTS

Jane took her religion seriously. There was family worship in the mornings, prayers in the evening, and weekly church attendance. Jane read her children Bible stories and taught them to sing hymns. Supposedly Benjamin had some religious experiences before his death.

A clergyman, Reverend Fuller, wrote what is considered the most accurate account of the death of young Benjamin

Pierce. Fuller was one of about forty passengers in the same car as the Pierce family. He explained: "The coupling which joined our car with the other broke, and our car was whirled violently round so as to reverse ends, and we were swung down the rocky ledge. For once, I had no hope of escaping death."

It is said that the car rolled twice over the rocks and then splintered. Those who were only bruised worked long into the night to offer help to other passengers. Reverend Fuller noted particularly a mother who was badly burned but grateful that her child was alive. He continues:

> But a few steps from her, I saw the most appalling scene of all. There was another mother, whose agony passes beyond any description. She could shed no tears, but, overcome with grief, uttered such affecting words as I can never forget. It was Mrs. Pierce, the wife of the President-elect; and near her in the ruin of shivered glass and iron, lay a more terrible ruin—her only son, one minute before so beautiful, so full of life and hope. . . . Sacred is the holy privacy of sorrow, and the hearts of those who have suffered can feel what my pen may not describe.

Benjamin had been struck in the forehead with such force that his skull had split, covering his face with blood. Jane never was able to move beyond her grief—forever robbed of peace and emotional strength.

In a letter to her sister, she wrote:

> The last two nights my dear boy has been in my dreams with peculiar vividness. May God forgive this aching yearning that I feel so much. . . . Little interruptions are very abundant here, and I do not accomplish half I wish to, either in reading or writing. I came accidentally upon some of my precious child's things, but I was obliged to turn and seem interested in other things.

Jane stopped the Saturday night marine band concerts, since they coincided and interfered with her prayer hours. Black fabric was placed in the staterooms of the White House. Slowly Jane began to rationalize that her precious son was taken that fateful day so that her husband would have no distractions. Understandably, this caused her to blame her husband somewhat for the death of their precious son—had Franklin not been in politics, Benjamin would not have been on that train.

Julia Dent Grant

1826-1902

The only way to get along is to take the world as you find it and make the best of it.

JULIA GRANT

God is not unjust; he will not forget your work and the love you have shown him as you have helped his people and continue to help them. We want each of you to show this same diligence to the very end, in order to make your hope sure.

HEBREWS 6:10–11

LIFE AND TIMES

The success of Julia Dent's marriage to Ulysses S. Grant may best be shown by the sentence she wrote about him in her memoirs, years after her husband's death: "The light of his glorious fame still reaches out to me, falls upon me, and warms me."

Raised on a plantation in Missouri, Julia Dent was surrounded by the Southern lifestyle—wealth for the white landowners, produced through the work of slaves. She attended The Misses Mauros' Boarding School in St. Louis for several years, refining her social graces and becoming well known in the city as a favorite belle. One day her brother, a student at West Point, brought home a classmate by the name of Hiram Grant. He insisted she call him Ulysses, and she began referring to her new friend as Ulys. He was awkward; she was gracious. He was quiet; she was talkative. They became fast friends. After he went away, the two exchanged frequent letters. She told him she dreamed of him, and he asked her to wear his West Point ring.

Julia's father objected to the marriage on account of Ulysses' poor background, but they were engaged in 1844. The war with Mexico delayed their marriage four years, but eventually the couple wed and Julia began a career of following after her military husband, moving from place to place, generally surrounded by rough men and few social events. After four years of marriage, Ulysses was ordered to the far western United States, and Julia moved back in with her parents, the West being no place for a lady. They both hated the separation, so Grant resigned his commission and decided to work for himself. He failed at farming, then failed at printing, then failed at running his own business. The family, now with four children, eventually moved back to Ulysses' hometown of Galena, Illinois, where he worked at his father's leather-goods store. When the Civil War broke out, Ulysses was given a commission with an Illinois regiment. That started a long, slow climb to fame as the commander of all Union forces.

His victories brought the couple to prominence and into social and political circles. When Ulysses was sworn in as President of the United States in 1869, Julia recorded that it launched "the happiest period of my life." She entertained lavishly and extensively, and her hospitality was much admired and similar to that of the earlier First Ladies. After eight years in office, the Grants toured the world and visited with the wealthy and powerful, often the guests of honor at lavish parties.

However, some poor business decisions and some untrustworthy friends caused the couple to lose nearly everything they had. At the same time, Ulysses was diagnosed with throat cancer. Determined to provide for his wife, he began writing about his life, thus creating the most famous presidential memoir in history. Helped by his friend Mark Twain, he completed the work just before he died. Sales of the book restored the family's fortune and provided for Julia until her death.

A few years before her death, Julia penned her own memoirs, recounting the joys and tragedies she had experienced in that remarkable period in American history. Her book remained unpublished until 1975, but when it was released, the world once again could see the love and respect the Grants had for each other. Her admiration for her husband and her willingness to stand by him when things weren't going well speak volumes for her character and fortitude.

INTERESTING FACTS

It's not generally known that Julia Grant joined her husband on the battlefield, often near the fighting, because they couldn't bear to be apart for long. Grant's aide-de-camp said, concerning their loving ways, "They would seek a quiet corner of his quarters of an evening, and sit with her hand in his, manifesting the most ardent devotion; and if a staff-officer came accidentally upon them they would look as bashful as two young lovers spied upon in the scenes of their courtship."

At one point Ulysses ordered Julia to stop nursing ill soldiers because she brought so many requests to him for her recovering patients to be discharged from the Union Army.

In the White House Julia took her job as hostess seriously. She lived to entertain, or so it seems. She was praised for her lively dinners, which were pleasant and added much to the somber society following the Civil War. She held weekly receptions that were truly "republican" gatherings, which meant anyone who wanted to come was welcome. She delighted in being kind to all. Social observer Benjamin Perley Poore wrote:

> There were ladies from Paris in elegant attire and ladies from the interior in calico, ladies whose cheeks were tinged with rouge, and others whose faces were weather-bronzed by outdoor work; ladies as lovely as Eve, and others as naughty as Mary Magdalene; ladies in diamonds, and others in dollar jewelry; chambermaids elbowed countesses, and all enjoyed themselves.

The Grants were affectionate with one another and also with their children. George W. Childs, editor of the *Philadelphia Ledger*, claimed he hadn't seen a "greater case of domestic happiness than existed in the Grant family." The four children adored their parents.

There are many instances where the Grants were playful, teasing and having fun together. They brought out the best in one another, it was said. For example, Julia helped her husband converse, since he was at times criticized for being too quiet. Her method?

> I would begin to tell something with which I knew he was perfectly familiar and would purposely tell it all wrong. Then the General would say, "Julia, you are telling that all wrong," and seemed quite troubled at my incompetency. I would innocently ask, "Well, how was it then?" He would begin, tell it all so well, and for the remainder of the evening would be so brilliant and so deeply interesting.

Julia was a Methodist and always attended church. During the around-the-world trip the Grants took after they left the

White House, they fulfilled Julia's lifelong dream by visiting the Holy Land. Julia said she felt the presence of God in the Garden of Gethsemane as she prayed.

When Queen Victoria was explaining to Mrs. Grant the trials of her many duties, Julia replied, "Yes, I can imagine them. I too have been the wife of a great ruler."

In 1897 Julia Grant actually attended the opening ceremonies at Grant's Tomb in New York's Central Park. Grant had died several years earlier, and the tomb was built for both of them. Julia attended the festivities and joked about how she wasn't ready to go. She died in 1902.

Lucy Ware Webb Hayes

1831-1889

But I must close—God grant to spare you all. Our boys pray fervently for the Reg. that they "may not be killed that the brave men—our men—who are fighting for our flag—may not be wounded—and if they are killed we know oh Lord they are with them in Heaven"—this has been part of Birchie's prayer for three or four weeks—those that die he knows are with Jesus—well his mother feels like the boy.

LUCY, TO HER HUSBAND, MAY 24, 1862

This morning I went to hear Rev Mr Trimble preach—taking Birch and little Rud with me—no church at the Episcopal so Fannie went also—the sermon was very good—the little boys behaved so well—that I felt quite happy—but then when all is pleasant and happy around me—the desire is with me so earnest and anxious—that I was only a true Christian.

I try to read my bible and pray for the safety of those dear to me—but of myself all is rain and cold—What would I not give to feel and view things as Mrs Dr Davis—to her the future is all peace and joy—I can never talk to any one of these things—not even to you—and so I grope along at times trying so earnestly—then again indifferent—I almost despair of ever being what I so earnestly desire.

LUCY, TO HER HUSBAND, AUGUST 30, 1863

LIFE AND TIMES

Lucy Hayes was one of the best loved First Ladies of all time, but she had an uphill battle to be accepted in that role. Her husband, Rutherford B. Hayes, had not won a clear-cut majority, and when the couple left their Ohio home for the inauguration in March 1877, the outcome of the election was still in doubt. Votes by the Senate and Supreme Court determined the outcome in her husband's favor, but it was clear that many Americans doubted Hayes had actually won the election. There was no inaugural ball scheduled, and the American public wasn't sure what to make of this Ohio lawyer and his wife.

Born in a small town in Ohio, Lucy had lost her father at the age of two and had taken on the responsibility for her own education, graduating from Ohio Wesleyan University at eighteen, after having taken a full load of classes—something generally reserved only for male students. She was the first of the First Ladies to hold an earned college degree.

Rutherford Hayes, whom she called Rud, had noticed her immediately after setting up his law practice in Cincinnati. He was impressed with her intellect, her honesty, and her "low, sweet voice." They were married in 1852, and the couple shared a deep conviction that slavery was immoral in the eyes of God. Throwing themselves into their church and community, the couple had eight children and became leaders in their community.

71

During the Civil War, Rutherford became a commander in the Ohio Volunteer Infantry, and Lucy was recognized and appreciated by his men for ministering to the wounded and encouraging the homesick. His distinguished combat record led to Rutherford's being elected to the United States Congress, then later to three terms as Governor of Ohio. During that time, people began to call her "Mother Lucy," and she was known to have a strong social conscience, visiting schools, prisons, army encampments, and even asylums. She became perhaps the most revered First Lady in Ohio's history.

After Rutherford took office, many in Washington began to appreciate Lucy's intelligence and political acumen. It was clear that her happy home life had given her the confidence to welcome those from every corner of American life, and she was known to spare no expense in bringing order and happiness to the White House. When inevitable criticism came her way, Lucy took it in good humor, earning the nickname "Lemonade Lucy" in the press for her ability to take lemons and turn them into lemonade. She became an outspoken advocate of women's rights and temperance in her era, though always with grace and an obvious respect for her husband's position. She was known for her gentle wisdom, even temper, and creative flair.

Her husband served only one term as President, deciding not to seek reelection. Instead, they moved back to their estate in Ohio, known as Spiegel Grove, and spent the next several years actively involved in their church and community. Lucy died just before the new century dawned, and just days before she died, she was still advocating for stronger rights for women.

INTERESTING FACTS

Lucy first met her future husband when she was fourteen and he was twenty-three. They were not interested in each other then, but their mothers thought they would make a good match. Hayes later visited Lucy in college when he was starting his law practice in Cincinnati. They went to poetry readings, lectures, and picnics, and her name began to appear more and more frequently in his diary. They were engaged a year and a half before they were married in her mother's parlor on December 30, 1852.

If ever we are again united—it shall be my earnest constant effort to be more deserving of your love— to be more necessary to your happiness than ever— I often think of the happy future—when once more a family together—our boys loving and honoring us— and think of bright happy days—God grant we may be together in old age—yes darling—I am getting older—but it [sic] so strange I cannot feel more than a little girl—when you first saw me and then when you loved me—But good bye dearest.

LUCY, IN A LETTER TO HER HUSBAND, AUGUST 29, 1862

Mrs. Hayes started what has become a tradition. When the children of Washington were prevented from rolling their Easter eggs on the Capitol grounds, Lucy invited them to use the White House lawn on the Monday following Easter. Her young adult nieces and cousins were often guests at the White House, assisting in the hosting of White House social functions.

By the end of Rutherford's term in office, Lucy was acclaimed the "most widely known and popular President's wife the country has known."

There were jokes about her temperance—"Water flowed like wine in the Hayes's White House." But actually the temperance stance was Rutherford's decision, which Lucy supported. The only time they served wine was for the April 1877 reception for the Grand Dukes Alexis and Constantine, sons of Tsar Alexander II of Russia.

Everyday life in the White House followed a pleasant routine and became a good example of Christian morality. After breakfast and a walk through the greenhouses, the family and guests gathered in the library where a chapter from the Bible was read and the Lord's Prayer repeated. Sunday evening soirees in the White House parlor were instituted by the Hayes family. At these times the family would gather around the piano, and Lucy would lead the singing of hymns, particularly favorites such as "Jesus, Lover of My Soul" and "Blest Be the Tie That Binds."

While the Hayeses were living there, the White House was home to a mockingbird, two dogs, a goat, and the nation's first Siamese cat. Spiegel Grove also housed many pets.

Mrs. Hayes was very attentive to the needs of those who were less fortunate than she. While First Lady, she was known to spend nine hundred dollars a month on the homeless.

When the couple celebrated their twenty-fifth wedding anniversary, the national press hailed Lucy as "representing the new woman era." Lucy wore her original wedding gown when they renewed their vows—remarkable since she had given birth to eight children!

Frances Folsom Cleveland

1864-1947

She carries sunshine wherever she goes.

TRIBUTE TO FRANCES CLEVELAND

But the fruit of the Spirit is love, joy, peace, patience, kindness, goodness, faithfulness, gentleness and self-control.

GALATIANS 5:22–23

LIFE AND TIMES

Frances Cleveland, the first woman to be married in the White House, was known for her youthful beauty and widely considered the first "modern" woman to serve as First Lady.

Born in Buffalo, New York, Frances was the daughter of a lawyer who died while she was still a girl. Her father's law partner, Grover Cleveland, who had actually purchased her first baby carriage, looked after the young Frances after the death of her father. He suggested she attend Wells College to make sure she received a solid education, and he even kept her room filled with flowers as a means of encouraging her during her studies.

After Frances graduated, Grover corresponded with her on a weekly basis, after receiving permission from Frances's mother. At the time, he was an important figure in politics and eventually elected President. It was during one of her visits to the White House in late 1885 that Frances and Grover began courting, and they were wed on the lawn of the President's home on June 2, 1886.

She was young and beautiful. He was twenty-seven years older. Grover's sister had served as the White House hostess during Grover's first year in office, but that role was quickly assumed by Frances, whom Grover called Frank. Her beauty and charm brought both of them immediate popularity with the American public. She began hosting two receptions each week—one during the week for visiting dignitaries and one on weekends to which she invited workingwomen. She firmly believed that those hardworking women who were never able to attend White House receptions during the week should have the opportunity, so she held the Saturday receptions.

Their social popularity did not bring about political victory, however, and Grover lost his bid for reelection in 1889. The couple moved to New York and continued to be the darlings of the society pages. When their daughter Ruth was born, it spawned the Baby Ruth phenomenon. The child is said to have been the inspiration for the candy bar called Baby Ruth, which was introduced in 1893, when Ruth was not yet two years old.

To date, Grover Cleveland is the only United States President to serve two separate terms. He was reelected in 1893. During this second time in the White House, the family received extensive newspaper coverage, because baby Esther was born. The couple had five children in all, three daughters and two sons. After Grover's death in 1908, Frances wore mourning dress for a full four years. On February 10, 1913, she married Thomas Jex Preston, an archaeology professor. When Frances died in 1947, she was buried next to Grover Cleveland and her daughter Ruth, who died in 1904.

INTERESTING FACTS

A Presbyterian, Frances was committed to charity and temperance. For many years following her time in the White House, she served as president of the Needlework Guild of America (NGA)—an organization that helped sew and distribute nearly two million garments during the years of the Depression. Though not politically involved in social issues, she did small things, such as listing the price for seamstresses to help prevent their being cheated by wealthy women who didn't want to pay the going rate.

Frances strongly believed in Sunday being a day of rest and, while in the White House, she decreed that no work should be done on that day.

In 1888, during her husband's second bid for the presidency, rumors persisted that Frances was being physically abused by her husband—even pamphlets circulated at the Democratic Convention made this claim! Local pastors and newspapers agreed. Frances was quite distressed by the publicity, and this led to her husband's eventual purchase of Red Top, a home in Chevy Chase, where the family spent most of their time during the second term of Grover's presidency to escape the public eye.

In an effort to stop the charges she viewed as outrageous, Frances responded by issuing a letter to the press that was published by the New York *Evening Post* on June 6, 1888:

I can only say . . . I pity the man who has been made the tool to give circulation to such wicked and heartless lies. I can wish the women of our country no better blessing than that their homes and their lives may be as happy, and that their husbands may be as kind and attentive, as considerate and affectionate, as mine.

When she was asked whether she would want to be the First Lady again, she replied, "What! There where my husband was accustomed to drag me about the house by the hair and where my children were blind, deaf, and deformed? Never!"

Perhaps more than any other family before them, the Clevelands suffered from a public that was thoroughly enamored with their children, to the point that security became an issue. On one occasion Frances looked out the window and saw her young baby Ruth being passed around by a group of complete strangers while the baby's nurse was helpless to stop them. And it is said that several times tourists had to be restrained from cutting a lock of baby Ruth's hair as the baby's nurse carried her around the White House. The gates to the grounds of the White House were eventually closed to the public because there was no other adequate way to protect the family.

Caroline Lavinia Scott Harrison

1832-1892

Yet with the faith she knew
We see her still
Even as here she stood—
All that was pure and good
And sweet in womanhood—
God's will her will.

WRITTEN BY JAMES WHITCOMB RILEY, AN INDIANA POET,
ON THE OCCASION OF MRS. HARRISON'S DEATH

He saved us through the washing of rebirth and renewal by the Holy Spirit, whom he poured out on us generously through Jesus Christ our Savior, so that, having been justified by his grace, we might become heirs having the hope of eternal life. . . . And I want you to stress these things, so that those who have trusted in God may be careful to devote themselves to doing what is good. These things are excellent and profitable for everyone.

TITUS 3:5–8

79

LIFE AND TIMES

Born in Oxford, Ohio, in 1832, Caroline Scott was the daughter of John Witherspoon Scott, a Presbyterian pastor and teacher and also the founder of the Oxford Female Institute. Carrie was cute, petite, smart, and known for her independent ways. She enjoyed dancing and popular music, though her Presbyterian church frowned on both, and she loved painting and was an accomplished artist. She was also completely in love with Benjamin Harrison, an honor student at Miami University of Ohio. After Ben graduated, the couple was married. They lived with his family in North Bend, Ohio, before moving to Indiana.

Carrie, as her husband called her, stood by Ben as he struggled in the early years of his career. But he found success as a Civil War general, and that translated into political success after the war. As Ben became deeply involved in politics, Carrie cared for their two children and was active in her church. She spent time working at a home for orphans, was known for her hospitality to friends, and continued her interest in both art and dance.

Unfortunately, when her husband was elected to the United States Senate, Carrie was struggling with health issues that kept her from moving to Washington. She was thrilled when he moved home after his six-year term ended and perhaps less thrilled when, two years later, he was elected President. But 1889 was the centennial of George Washington's inauguration, and the country was suddenly interested in history, so Carrie dutifully threw herself into the role of First Lady.

She helped found the National Society of the Daughters of the American Revolution (DAR), an organization that would grow to become influential and still be popular in many areas of the country today. She volunteered to be the organization's first president, and that experience sparked in her an interest in the history of the White House and the role of First Lady.

We have within ourselves the only element of destruction; our foes are from within, not from without. Our hope is in unity and self-sacrifice.

FROM CARRIE'S ADDRESS TO THE FIRST CONTINENTAL CONGRESS OF
THE DAUGHTERS OF THE AMERICAN REVOLUTION

Out of her research came a renewal of many old traditions, as well as the creation of several new ones. She was the first to establish a White House archive and to create a collection of White House china. She was also one of the first women in the national media to promote women's rights and to openly advocate for a woman's right to attend the college of her choice.

What have we ever done that we should be held up to ridicule by newspapers . . . cruelly attacked . . . made fun of, for the country to laugh at! If this is the penalty . . . I hope the Good Lord will deliver my husband from any further experience.

CAROLINE, AFTER HER HUSBAND WAS ATTACKED
AND HUMILIATED BY THE PRESS

While the Harrisons lived in the White House, their children and grandchildren lived with them. The crowded home caused Carrie to try unsuccessfully to get Congress to fund a renovation and enlargement of the President's mansion. She wanted the White House to have up-to-date improvements, believing that the President's family influenced the rest of American culture. Carrie understood that the way she and her family lived in the White House would set the tone for the rest of the country to follow.

Over time, it became clear that Carrie's health was deteriorating, but she continued to serve as hostess at elegant government receptions. Other women in Washington society circles noted that her fun-loving spirit seemed to diminish, though her dignity and charm continued to be appreciated by all who visited the White House during her husband's administration. By the winter of 1892, it was clear Carrie was seriously ill with tuberculosis, and she withdrew from public life. She died in October of that year and was buried at her home church in Indianapolis. Carrie Harrison would long be remembered as a woman ahead of her time and one who had influenced the public's perception of the role of First Lady.

INTERESTING FACTS

While living in Indianapolis, the Harrisons' lives revolved around the preaching and activities of the First Presbyterian Church. Following her husband's return from the Union Army, Carrie taught the Sunday school class for toddlers, while her husband taught a class for young men. Mrs. Harrison also served as a mentor for the younger women in the church, and both she and her husband served on the missionary society.

While First Lady, Carrie was approached to help with a fund-raising event for Johns Hopkins University medical school. Carrie agreed to lend her name and influence but only if they would start admitting women to their program.

Johns Hopkins agreed, changed their policies, and watched with delight as Mrs. Harrison successfully raised half a million dollars for the medical school.

Carrie became known for the many plants she brought into the White House. She was especially fond of orchids and tended her plants in the greenhouses, bringing many into the White House. When the Clevelands returned for their second term, the rooms were bursting with flowers. One visitor described the East Room: "About a mile of smilax for chandelier festoons; and on the mantels and window seats elsewhere, 5,000 azalea blossoms, 800 carnations, 300 roses, 300 tulips, 900 hyacinths, 400 lilies of the valley, 200 bouvardias, 100 sprays of asparagus ferns, 40 heads of poinsettia, and 200 small ferns."

Throughout her life, Carrie loved to paint and also enjoyed making china surfaces to paint. She had a kiln and made literally hundreds of projects both for gifts and church bazaars. She invited women into the White House for lessons in painting as well as French lessons, and she sent many gifts out in response to letters, which often announced that babies had been born and named for the President.

A tapestry of goodness, charity, and devotion.

TRIBUTE TO CAROLINE HARRISON

Edith Kermit Carow Roosevelt

1861-1948

I think the petition in the Litany, "Strengthen those who
stand, comfort the weak-hearted, raise up those who fall,
and finally beat down Satan under our feet" is especially
for boys going out into the big world. I had added it to
my prayers.

EDITH ROOSEVELT, REFLECTING ON THE LIVES OF HER FOUR BOYS

I do not think my eyes are blinded by affection when I
say that she has combined to a degree I have never seen
in any other woman the power of being best of wives and
mothers, the wisest manager of the household, and at
the same time the ideal great lady and mistress of the
White House.

THEODORE ROOSEVELT

LIFE AND TIMES

Edith Kermit Carow, or Edie, is one of the most interesting of all First Ladies. She had known Theodore Roosevelt
from childhood. As children they had played together in New

York, and the two had spent a considerable amount of time in each other's homes. While attending finishing school as a teen, she would often go to outings as Theodore's friend and companion, but the two drifted apart when he went off to Harvard.

Teddy, as she called him, married the former Alice Hathaway Lee in 1880, and Edith attended the wedding as a friend of the family. But Alice Roosevelt died just five years later, leaving Teddy a widower with an infant daughter. Very shortly after the funeral, Edith and Teddy once again struck up their friendship, and just before Christmas in 1886, the couple married in London, England.

They settled into a house in Oyster Bay, New York, and had five children in ten years. During that time, the energetic Teddy served in numerous influential positions in government yet always seemed to make time for his wife and children. They were a close-knit family, known for having much activity in their lives, and Edith was as active as any. They took trips and hikes together, sometimes over rough ground, and everyone was expected to keep up with Theodore, the former soldier. He regaled his family with stories of his adventures around the world, and Edith was known to enjoy her husband's stories immensely, though she had doubtless heard them many times. And Edith made sure the family remained very involved in their church, particularly in efforts to help those less fortunate than themselves.

In 1900 some Republican leaders, in an attempt to move the popular Teddy out of the public eye, suggested he be moved from the Governor's office in New York to the role of Vice President to William McKinley. They thought the job would keep Roosevelt busy but away from the press and any important roles. Just six months after McKinley's reelection, he was assassinated, and Teddy Roosevelt became President of the United States.

On moving into the White House, Edith declared she would maintain her family's privacy, and she worked hard to keep reporters from finding out about herself and her children. That meant the public knew little of Edith's wisdom and energy, particularly of her frequent sessions in which she shared her ideas and perspective with the President.

I suppose in a short time I shall adjust myself to this, but the horror of it hangs over me, and I am never without fear for Theodore. The Secret Service men follow him everywhere. I try and comfort myself with the line of the old hymn, "Brought safely by His hand thus far, why should we now give place to fear?"

EDITH, AFTER HER HUSBAND TOOK THE OATH OF OFFICE, FOLLOW-
ING THE ASSASSINATION OF PRESIDENT MCKINLEY

There were dinner parties that brought together the best and brightest minds of the day, and Edith was as involved in the conversations as anyone. She read extensively, wanting to understand the important ideas and current philosophies. Those who knew the family recognized that she brought practicality and a deflating sense of wit to her husband's more exotic tendencies. Edith was smart and well bred but always considerate of others. Teddy considered her his wisest counselor.

Her husband served two terms as President, went into retirement, then nearly won a third term when he returned to public life as the Bull Moose party candidate. After he passed away in 1919, Edith continued to travel and read widely. She remained committed to assisting the poor and eventually helped start the Needlework Guild of America, a charity that provided garments for the poor, and she volunteered regularly at Christ Church in Oyster Bay.

Edith lost three of her four sons to war, and she outlived her husband by nearly thirty years. She died on September 30, 1948, at the age of eighty-seven. Her wishes for her funeral included a simple coffin, a crepe shawl of her own if there was no church pall, and only pink and blue flowers on the coffin, with instructions for the music, which included "Love Divine" and "The Son of God."

INTERESTING FACTS

Edith and her husband did not attend the same church. She and the children went to an Episcopal church, while Theodore preferred the denomination he grew up in, Dutch Reformed. If a child was naughty during service, it was expected that the offender would be spending the following Sunday with his father.

Throughout their time in the White House, Edith spent thirty minutes reading and talking with her children before dinner each evening. Often Teddy would join them; he also liked to listen to her read. When she was finished, it was time for his activity of choice—wrestling with the children on the floor.

The Roosevelt family had a number of pets, including guinea pigs, lizards, a kangaroo rat that was fed sugar cubes at the breakfast table, and a young black bear that the children called Jonathan Edwards. Theodore claimed in his *Autobiography* that this name for the bear was chosen "partly out of compliment to their mother, who was descended from that great Puritan divine, and partly because the bear possessed a temper in which gloom and strength were combined in what the children regarded as Calvinistic proportions."

Other pets were General Grant, the pony; Emily Spinach, the snake; Eli the macaw; Loretta the parrot; as well as dogs and cats. There was even a pet cemetery of sorts behind the White House during the Roosevelts' time there, although Edith had its contents exhumed when they left office.

While in the White House, Edith established the Ladies Picture Gallery. She also made use of a social secretary, the first of the First Ladies to do so. With her young family, she did not have a very large political role. However, she was critical of other politicians, particularly any man who was believed to be a womanizer.

Ellen Louise Axson Wilson

1860-1914

I wonder how anyone who reaches middle age can bear it if she cannot feel on looking back that, whatever mistakes she may have made, she has on the whole lived for others and not for herself.

ELLEN WILSON

LIFE AND TIMES

Ellen Axson grew up in Rome, Georgia, and first came into contact with her future husband when she was a baby and he was only six. Supposedly the two did not meet again till Thomas Woodrow Wilson was a young lawyer. Not surprisingly, they met at church, since both were children of Presbyterian ministers. Wilson was in love with the gorgeous Ellen in short order. She called him Tommy; he called her Miss Ellie Lou, and the couple were engaged while she was still a teenager.

Ellen was the eldest of seven children. Her mother, Margaret Hoyt Axson, died during the birth of Ellen's youngest sibling in 1881, when Ellen was twenty-one years old. The death of his wife caused Ellen's father to suffer a severe depression, so Ellen cared for her ailing father until he passed away in 1884, when she became the head of the family.

What a bright, pretty face, what splendid, mischievous laughing eyes! I'll lay a wager that this demure little lady has lots of life and fun in her!

WOODROW WILSON, RECALLING HIS FIRST THOUGHTS OF ELLEN

In 1885, after they were married, the Wilsons and Ellen's youngest brother moved to Bryn Mawr College, where Wilson had been offered a teaching job. When Ellen became pregnant, she made sure that she traveled back to Georgia to remain with relatives for the delivery, so that her children (three daughters) would not be born Yankees. Woodrow later moved on to Wesleyan University, then to a role at Princeton. Ellen, who was painfully shy, found herself forced into uncomfortable social responsibilities because of her husband's career. She found her refuge in art, which she had studied briefly while living in New York. Compared with professional art of that time, her paintings were of good quality, and as her husband gained national recognition, she spent more and more time in her studio, enjoying the quiet.

Woodrow Wilson's first political office was that of Governor of New Jersey. When he ran for President in 1912, it was a three-way race because Teddy Roosevelt had returned to politics as the Bull Moose party candidate. Wilson was elected with a mere 42 percent of the popular vote. The circumstances of the election threw the Wilsons into the spotlight, causing

Ellen great discomfort. In 1913, to retreat from the public, she had a skylight installed in an upper room at the White House (the first skylight in the President's mansion) and turned the room into a studio for her painting. Over time she became a bit more comfortable in her role as America's hostess, particularly when two of her daughters were married in the White House. Still, she once said of herself that she was "the most unambitious of women" and admitted she had no interest in the role of First Lady.

Mrs. Wilson survived the receptions and parties by being cordial yet plain. She insisted to her husband they not have an inaugural ball, so they held a private dinner with a small group of influential legislators instead. (That decision led to the passage of an important tariff bill, thereby pleasing her husband and dimming some of the criticism from the Washington press.) Ellen and Woodrow spent many evenings together, reading Dickens or Wordsworth aloud.

The combination of bad press, the pressure of her role, and her own introverted nature caused Ellen to suffer several maladies, including a growing problem with her kidneys. Her health slowly failed, and she died on August 6, 1914, after only two years in Washington. The nation mourned as the President returned her body to Rome, Georgia, to be buried among her kin.

INTERESTING FACTS

Ellen was active in service as a young woman. She volunteered two nights a week at a missionary school while attending art school in New York. She had a heart for others and was an active hostess during her time in Princeton. She was known for her warm nature.

The one thing Ellen found she could throw herself into as First Lady was the cause of the poor, particularly the African American population that filled Washington's slums. Though a descendant of slave owners, she nevertheless lent her name and prestige to the cause of social justice and brought much attention to the plight of Blacks and the dilapidated inner cities.

Ellen worked tirelessly to promote her cause, designing legislation to help provide adequate housing for the poorest residents of Washington, D.C. For her actions and care of those in the slums, she earned the name "Angel in the White House." Her bill, officially called Mrs. Wilson's bill, passed while Ellen was on her deathbed in August 1914. While the legislation cleared the slums, it didn't fully tell how new housing would come about for those who had lived there. Her contribution was significant because she was the first among the First Ladies to have a social cause. In some sense, she set a precedent, doing more than the charity efforts and good deeds of the First Ladies who preceded her.

On her tombstone was written:

> *A traveller between life and death*
> *The reason firm. The temperate will*
> *Endurance, foresight, strength and skill*
> *A perfect woman nobly planned*
> *To warn, to comfort and command*
> *And yet a spirit still and bright*
> *With something of angelic light.*

Grace Anna
Goodhue Coolidge

1879-1957

The Open Door

You, my son
Have shown me God.
Your kiss upon my cheek
Has made me feel the gentle touch
Of Him who leads us on.
The memory of your smile, when young,
Reveals His face,
As mellowing years come on apace.
And when you went before,
You left the gates of Heaven ajar,
That I might glimpse,
Approaching from afar,
The glories of His grace.
Hold, son, my hand,
Guide me along the path,
That, coming,
I may stumble not,
Nor roam,
Nor fail to show the way
Which leads us home.

GRACE COOLIDGE, WRITTEN AFTER HER SON CALVIN'S DEATH,
PUBLISHED IN *GOOD HOUSEKEEPING* IN 1929

Your note of sympathy and understanding helps the President and me and I am writing to tell you so. We had great hope that Calvin would recover up to the very last for he fought valiantly. It was not for our human understanding to comprehend His plan. I can only bow my head and thank Him for having loaned him to me for sixteen years and ask Him for strength equal to his faith.

GRACE COOLIDGE, TO FORMER FIRST LADY EDITH WILSON

LIFE AND TIMES

In 1931 Grace Coolidge was voted one of "America's twelve greatest living women." She once received a gold medal from the National Institute of Social Sciences for her "fine personal influence exerted as First Lady"—a remarkable tribute, considering the fact that her husband left office with limited respect.

Growing up in a small town in Vermont, Grace Goodhue had a heart for other people. As an only child, she was fun loving and gained an appreciation for deaf children at an early age. While a student at the University of Vermont in the early 1900s, she heard about a school for deaf children and decided to get a degree that would allow her to teach deaf students. In the fall of 1902, she took a job at the Clarke School for the Deaf. Not much later she met Calvin Coolidge through the Congregational church, and the couple began dating. They were married in her parents' home, and they lived in one-half of a duplex, counting their pennies as they began their family.

Calvin was a shy, quiet man, but Grace was outgoing and friendly. She made sure they participated in church activities, became part of the town's social circle, and had friends over regularly. She was active, and the neighbors noticed it was Grace who played baseball with the boys and made efforts to keep up appearances. Even as her husband ran for office, rising to be elected Governor of Massachusetts, she was the one who kept up their home, while Calvin skimped by on a dollar-and-a-half rented room in Boston.

In 1921, as wife of the Vice President, Grace Coolidge went from poor homemaker to Washington society woman—and she quickly became the most popular woman in the capital. Her obvious zest for life and her love of adventure charmed even the most cynical newspaper writer, and her simple-yet-stylish way set the tone for a country looking to Washington for leadership in all things cultural.

When President Warren G. Harding died, Grace planned the new administration's social life. It was dignified yet unpretentious—exactly what her reserved husband wanted. She was celebrated for her friendliness and simple ways, while being appreciated for her generosity and fashion sense. Throughout her husband's presidency, she was admired for both her tact and gaiety, which made her one of the most popular hostesses who had lived in the White House. In 1929 she left Washington with the country's respect and love.

Grace and Calvin suffered a tragic loss when their son Calvin Jr. died after a blister he got while playing tennis on the White House courts became infected. He died of blood poisoning on July 7, 1924. Grace wrote several poems about her loss and handled it with great dignity, knowing that she was still needed in the White House. It's apparent from her poems that she recognized God's sovereignty through this tragedy.

After leaving the White House, the Coolidges bought a home they called The Beeches—a large house with grounds for parties. President Coolidge died there in 1933, but before he passed away, he paid tribute to Grace in his memoirs, saying most appropriately that he had always "rejoiced in her graces."

After her husband's death, Grace moved on to try many new adventures, such as riding in an airplane, taking a trip to Europe, and continuing to participate in her ministry to deaf students.

Grace Coolidge always seemed to keep a sense of fun, yet she was no publicity hound, and she admitted late in life that she'd never been comfortable as the center of attention. It was for that balance of adventure and humility that Americans loved her. She died in 1957, an inspiration to many.

INTERESTING FACTS

Grace joined the Congregational church when she was sixteen. Her father served as a deacon at the church and was known as the "handy deacon," since he knew how to repair the organ.

Calvin had strong opinions on what his wife should and should not do. Grace was forbidden to do a number of things, including conducting interviews, wearing culottes (the predecessor to women's pants), curling her hair, learning to drive, and flying in an airplane.

He encouraged her to wear pretty dresses—he even bought her clothes, which was saying a great deal since by nature he was quite thrifty.

Supposedly when Grace was posing for her first official portrait, with her white collie, Rob Roy, she was wearing a beautiful red dress. Her husband felt her white dress would be better. When the painter said he needed the contrast between the white dog and the suggested dress, Coolidge reportedly said, "No problem, just paint the dog red."

Grace is said to have accepted the restrictions her husband made while keeping a cheerful disposition, but it is also said that when she was upset and couldn't laugh it off or walk away, she turned to something else. "Many a time, when I have needed to hold myself firmly," she once admitted, "I have taken up my needle. It might be a sewing needle, knitting needles, or a crochet hook—whatever its form or purpose, it often proved to be as the needle of the compass, keeping me to the course."

Grace loved sports and could throw a baseball better than most men. She often attended games, especially of her beloved Boston Red Sox. When she couldn't go to games, she listened to them on the radio. Washington Senator and baseball player Bucky Harris once said, "All the Washington players knew her and spoke to her. She was the most rabid baseball fan I ever knew in the White House." She appears to have had some influence over her husband after all. When the game was tied in the middle of the 1924 World Series, Calvin stood up to leave. Grace asked indignantly, "Where do you think you're going? You sit down." And he did!

Grace, an avid hiker, made national headlines in 1927 when she became lost while hiking in the Black Hills with Secret Service agent Jim Haley. President Coolidge was furious when he heard about her being lost and fired Agent Haley. Defiantly, Grace maintained a relationship with Agent Haley and his family.

Grace was an animal lover and kept a raccoon named Rebecca and also her collie Rob Roy with her in the White House. The nickname given her by the White House staff was "Sunshine."

Following her husband's death, Grace began a new chapter in her life and started to write articles for magazines and to speak out on issues. She was always close to her son John and his family and especially enjoyed her grandchildren.

Watch-Fires

Love was not given the human heart
For careless dealing.

Its spark was lit that man
Might know Divine revealing.
Heaped up with sacrificial brands
The flame, in mounting,
Enkindles other hearts with love
Beyond the counting.
Reflecting back into each life,
These vast fires, glowing
Do then become the perfect love
Of Christ's bestowing.

GRACE COOLIDGE

Lou Henry Hoover

1875-1944

I know that if I should die, I can pray my soul to go over to my two dear little boys and to help and comfort their souls. Of course you can't see it or hear it. But sometimes you will know that I am there, because your own little soul inside you will feel nice and comfy and cozy, because my bigger, older one is cuddling it. And when you are in trouble, and call for me to come to help you, and pray God to give you more force, why I can come right to you and bring along the new force he is sending to you.

Lou Hoover, in a letter to her two sons just before World War I

Life and Times

Lou Henry Hoover was different from most of the First Ladies of the early twentieth century. Rather than being raised in a family with privilege, she was from a modest home, was plainspoken, and was a student long before her role insisted she become one.

When she was ten, Lou and her family moved to California from Iowa. She became a lover of the outdoors when her father began taking her camping in the San Gorgonio Mountains. She hunted, was a skilled horsewoman, and studied nature extensively. One day, while working in a geology lab as a student at Stanford University, she met Herbert Hoover, a senior student who shared her love of science. He was impressed with both her beauty and her mind, and they were married in 1899.

Immediately after their wedding, the couple left for China, where Herbert had a job as a mining engineer. From there they traveled around the globe to Thailand, Australia, Egypt, Japan, and several countries in Europe. They became wealthy, had two sons, and eventually became well known. Hoover ran an emergency relief program during World War I.

During the war years, Lou took the boys back to California and helped design a home for the family in Palo Alto. She also spent time with her husband, who was in London serving in the war relief effort. After the war her husband was chosen to be Secretary of Commerce, so the family moved to Washington D.C., where they spent the next eight years. It was during this time that Lou became an active leader in the Girl Scout movement, eventually becoming the president of the organization and leading it to worldwide prominence.

In 1929 the family moved to the White House, bringing with them considerable experience in public affairs both at home and abroad. Unfortunately, late that year the economy collapsed, and President Hoover would take much of the blame for the chaos that ensued.

But during their four years in the presidency, Lou Hoover brought her experience and charity to the task. She paid for the education of many poor children who could not afford schooling on their own. She restored Abraham Lincoln's study so that her husband could read his books in the same manner Lincoln, whom Herbert considered the greatest

President, had read his books. She used her own money to reproduce furniture used by President Monroe in the White House sitting room. And when the nation's economy grew weak, she insisted on using their own private funds to entertain guests at government social events. They entertained elegantly, and Lou was known for her lovely evening gowns and positive spirit in the midst of the country's adversity. At the end of their term, at the depth of the Depression in 1933, the Hoovers decided to forgo the traditional New Year's Day greeting of the public—Lou Hoover recognized her husband simply couldn't take the negative remarks he would have to face.

They retired to Palo Alto but maintained a New York apartment where they would spend time with friends and former colleagues. It wasn't until after her death that Lou Hoover would be recognized and appreciated for her charitable, giving character. In the words of her husband, she was a "symbol of everything wholesome in American life."

INTERESTING FACTS

After Lou married Herbert, she left the Episcopal Church and joined the Quakers.

During the First World War, the people of Belgium were in danger of starving. Because they were invaded without warning, and because most of the tiny population was within a territory controlled by the Germans and there was no international humanitarian relief program at this point, there was little anyone seemed able to do, but Lou did something. She worked at the Belgian Relief headquarters in London and even visited Belgium to see the situation for herself. She made speeches in the United States and worked to raise funds. Lou even persuaded the Rockefeller Foundation to provide free shipping for American clothes and food to be sent to the starving country.

Happily, Americans heard her cry. Thousands of fifty-pound bags of flour were sent to Belgium. The people of that country wanted to express their thanks, and despite the fact that many were living in poverty, they transformed, with the help of some intricate embroidery, some of those bags that had so enriched their country into pieces of artwork. It is said that Belgians were so grateful to the relief workers for their aid that those workers were treated like royalty.

No letup in food saving must be allowed.

There is some individual who is unknowingly

dependent upon you for life; maybe a soldier

in the trenches . . . or a peasant woman.

They will have nothing to eat next spring

if we do not think of them now.

LOU HOOVER

For her efforts, Lou was presented with the Cross Chevalier, Order of Leopold. And in response, she said, "What is there to say? I have done nothing extraordinary. . . ."

Lou helped countless people, with no fanfare or even the knowledge of the public. After her death, her husband discovered hundreds of instances of her aiding others of which he had not been aware.

As First Lady, Lou invited Mrs. Oscar DePriest, the wife of a Black congressman from Chicago, to tea. Not surprisingly, she was given terrible press from the Southern papers. However, her husband supported her. The following week he entertained a Black professor at lunch. Lou was a strong supporter of integration and invited the Tuskegee Institute choir to the White House to sing. Though much of the country supported her, there was great ridicule from the other end of the spectrum.

It isn't so important what others think of you as what you feel inside.

LOU HOOVER

Anna Eleanor Roosevelt

1884-1962

The only thing you can do for people is to love them and thereby give them a sense of security so that they know they can come to you and get understanding and forgiveness, even though they know that you disapprove of what they have done.

ELEANOR ROOSEVELT

LIFE AND TIMES

Eleanor Roosevelt, one of the most respected women of the twentieth century, started life as a shy child who needed love and recognition. Born in New York City in 1884, she was a niece of President Theodore Roosevelt but didn't have his passion for adventure or desire for greatness. Instead, she was awkward and lonely, having lost both her parents before the age of fifteen. Sent off to attend a finishing school in England, she discovered that being on her own helped her develop her self-confidence.

Tall and graceful, she made her debut at age seventeen, when she was introduced to her cousin Franklin Delano Roosevelt. They were engaged two years later and married two years after that. Theodore Roosevelt gave her away at her wedding. Over the next decade she would bear six children and become, in her own words, "a fairly conventional, quiet, young society matron."

All that changed when her husband was stricken with polio in 1921. Franklin had already begun a successful political career, and when he became sick, Eleanor stepped into his place. She became active in the New York Democratic Committee, helped him stay on top of the political decisions of the day, and nursed him back to health. When he ran for Governor, she was with him every day, becoming his eyes and ears among the people who would elect him.

In many ways, Eleanor Roosevelt dedicated her life to her husband's purposes. Though a powerful man, he was confined to a wheelchair, so she became the person who attended and reported on events for her husband. It gave her a unique perspective on the lives of average Americans, and when Franklin was elected to the White House in 1933, Eleanor probably had a better understanding of the social conditions in the country than any First Lady in history. She used her knowledge to transform the role of First Lady from "hostess" to "agent of change."

As First Lady, Eleanor broke precedent by speaking her mind publicly. She held press conferences, gave radio broadcasts, offered lectures on topics of the day, traveled around the country without her husband, and shared her honest opinions in a daily syndicated newspaper column "My Day." All of this made her a target for those who disliked her husband's political policies, but Eleanor's integrity and graciousness negated much of the criticism. She won fans by the millions, even in foreign countries, and became without question the best-known First Lady in history.

Though well known for her social work, Eleanor never shirked her official entertaining duties, greeting thousands of soldiers, statesmen, and visitors with charming friendliness. She took to heart the concerns of the common people;

at the height of the Depression she chose to cut costs for the Fourth of July capital dinner by serving hot dogs on the White House lawn. All of her decisions seemed to help her connect to Americans, who elected her husband to the presidency a record four times.

Adapting one's plans to the needs of others is what makes life worth living.

ELEANOR ROOSEVELT

After Franklin's death in 1945, Eleanor returned to a cottage at their Hyde Park estate. Soon she took up a role as American spokeswoman in the United Nations and continued an active career until her own death in 1962. She was honored by her beloved country when the flags at the Capitol were lowered to half-mast—another first for a First Lady. She is buried at Hyde Park beside her husband.

INTERESTING FACTS

Nicknames for Eleanor ranged from "Eleanor the Great" to "Stalin in Petticoats." No doubt these names were bestowed on her largely because of her outspoken nature and her willingness to act and never be intimidated. Other titles included "La Boca Grande" and "The Gab."

Sadly, the Roosevelts' marriage, though lasting, was not altogether happy. Around 1918 Franklin began an affair with Eleanor's social secretary. From that time forward, they never again lived as man and wife. To spare Franklin's career, Eleanor did not seek a divorce. They raised five children together (one died in infancy) and had a close partnership, as she liked to call it. "We understand that everything else depends upon the success of the wife and husband in their personal partnership relation."

Eleanor was a strong supporter of racial integration. In 1939 she shocked everyone when, after arriving at the organizational meeting of the Southern Conference on Human Welfare, she moved her chair into the middle of the aisle between the designated "white" and "Black" seating sections. When the Daughters of the American Revolution refused to allow Marian Anderson, a Black singer, to perform at a large auditorium in Washington, Eleanor resigned from the organization. (She also helped to organize an alternative concert for Ms. Anderson on the steps of the Lincoln Memorial.)

It was said that Eleanor never held still, even during conferences. She would pull out her knitting and work while she listened. She was, as one of her sons said, "a sort of roving one-woman task force for social reform and international good will." It is clear why she was often called First Lady of the world. People all over the world knew who she was.

Eleanor shared the burden of worry that many mothers and spouses experienced during World War II—all four of her sons joined the military to serve their country. Eleanor visited hospitals and wrote hundreds of letters to parents and spouses of soldiers in an effort to bring comfort.

You gain strength, courage and confidence
by every experience in which you
really stop to look fear in the face. . . .
You must do the thing you think you cannot do.

ELEANOR ROOSEVELT

Eleanor was a Presbyterian, but her religion tended to be a broad one of acceptance for all who desired to follow the Golden Rule. She attended church on a regular basis. Eleanor once said, "I sometimes think that the same spirit pervades the good people in all religions. If you want others to respect your beliefs, you must in return give respect for theirs."

There are many examples of Eleanor's tireless efforts on behalf of others. For example, every year she sent a check for ten dollars to the daughter of an acquaintance on the girl's birthday. The tradition had started during the Depression when she picked up a hitchhiker along the road and helped him find work. The man was so grateful that he promised that if he ever had a daughter, he would name her Eleanor. She replied that instead he should make her a godmother. He did just that. She mailed a last gift to the girl in 1962 and died the next day.

Elizabeth Virginia Wallace Truman

1885-1982

She [Elizabeth] saw that her mother's way of loving her father, the passive, tender but more or less mindless love of the genteel lady, was a mistake. It failed to share the bruises, the fears, the defeats a man experienced in his world. It left him exposed to spiritual loneliness. If she ever found a man she could trust . . . Bess Wallace vowed she would share his whole life, no matter how much pain it cost her.

MARGARET TRUMAN, *BESS TRUMAN*

He who finds a wife finds what is good
and receives favor from the LORD.
PROVERBS 18:22

Houses and wealth are inherited from parents,
but a prudent wife is from the LORD.
PROVERBS 19:14

109

LIFE AND TIMES

As a young child, Elizabeth Wallace was described as having "strong opinions . . . and no hesitation about stating them Missouri style—straight from the shoulder."

Elizabeth, affectionately nicknamed Bess, was born on February 13, 1885, to David and Margaret Gates Wallace. From fifth grade through high school, she attended the same school as Harry Truman, whose family had come to town in 1890. Harry always described her as having "golden curls" and "the most beautiful blue eyes," and their daughter once wrote a description of Bess as having been "a marvelous athlete—the best third baseman in Independence, a superb tennis player, a tireless ice skater—and she was pretty besides."

The first girl I ever knew who could whistle through her teeth and bat a ball as far as any boy in the neighborhood.

A FORMER CLASSMATE OF BESS

Before Lieutenant Truman left for France in 1918, Bess and Harry became engaged. In June of 1919 they were married, and their daughter, Mary Margaret, was born in 1924. Bess had suffered two miscarriages before their daughter was born. At this time the Trumans were living in Bess's childhood home, so they could care for her mother.

Harry would often refer to his wife as "the Boss" and liked to call his daughter "the Boss's Boss." After the war, he returned to civilian life as a war hero and haberdasher, and he began a career in local politics. Often Bess traveled with her husband and made platform appearances. When

Truman was elected to the United States Senate in 1934, the family moved to Washington.

Bess worked as Harry's secretary, and he once said she earned "every cent I paid her." She was reluctant to become a public figure, but in private she shared her husband's interests. Truman gained national recognition for his wartime chairmanship of a special committee on defense spending, which led to his becoming the fourth-term running mate of Democratic President Franklin Roosevelt. When the President died a mere three months after his fourth inauguration, Harry Truman took the President's oath of office.

Bess Truman became the new First Lady. Unfortunately, as Mr. Truman put it, she was not "especially interested" in the "formalities and pomp or the artificiality which, as we had learned . . . inevitably surround the family of the President." Also she was unhappy with the lack of privacy in the White House. She filled the social obligations of her position but did only what was absolutely necessary. During Truman's second term, the family lived in the Blair House during a much-needed restoration of the White House. This seemed to suit the down-home couple more than actually residing in the official mansion, because it allowed the Trumans to have a low-key social life.

On leaving office in 1953, the Trumans moved back to Independence. At first, neither knew what they would do, but soon both found that they could invest themselves in their community. When President Truman died in 1972, Bess remained living in the family home so she could entertain visits from family and friends. When she died in 1982, she was buried in the courtyard of the Harry S Truman Library beside her husband.

INTERESTING FACTS

From the beginning of Harry Truman's tenure as President, the press could not get a comment worth mentioning from Bess. She refused to speak with them on any matter and almost always responded to their questions with, "No comment." Her privacy was all-important to her. One *Newsweek* article in January 1946 reported: "Friends of Mrs. Truman insist that the country will love her when it comes to know her. But it seems very doubtful that Bess Truman, intent on being herself and upon seeing that her family has some privacy even in the White House, will ever give the country that chance."

Although known as "the Boss" to her husband, others called Bess "Payroll Bess" because she was a salaried member of Truman's staff during his tenure as a United States Senator. She had no problems with the arrangement and made it clear that the Truman family was not rich and had to work just like all the other families in America.

She was made of equal parts goodness and granite.

EDITH HELM, SECRETARY TO BESS

Bess Truman was a member of the Bible study that started the Community Services League, an organization that has been helping the needy since 1916. She became a member of the Congressional Club and the PEO Sisterhood. With the outbreak of World War II, she also became active in the H Street United Service Organization and in the Red Cross work of the Senate Wives Club.

Moving to the White House did not change Bess's routine. She continued to pay three dollars for a weekly manicure, shampoo, and set at her old beauty shop. She just rode there in her chauffeured limousine.

As First Lady, Mrs. Truman served as honorary president of the Girl Scouts, the Women's National Democratic Club, and the Washington Animal Rescue League. Bess was also an honorary chairman of the American Red Cross. The invitations to join the American Newspaper Women's Club, the Daughters of Colonial Wars, and the Women's National Farm and Garden Association indicate her popularity as First Lady. Several times during the 1950s Mrs. Truman's name appeared on the Gallup Poll's list of America's most admired women.

The Trumans' daughter, Margaret, in her book *Souvenir*, noted that writers had reported that her mother's favorite color was blue and that she preferred roses to any other flower, but the public wanted to know more.

My mother, whose public facade has been unvaryingly sedate and whose public utterances have been unfailingly courteous but cryptic, is perhaps the least understood member of our family. She is a woman of tremendous character, which the public may sense, but in addition she is a warmhearted, kind lady, with a robust sense of humor, a merry, twinkling wit, and a tremendous capacity for enjoying life.

Mamie Geneva
Doud Eisenhower

1896-1979

All I could do was pray without ceasing—just as I prayed for his father. Only with Johnnie, Ike prayed with me—and that helped.

MAMIE, WHEN HER OWN SON WAS IN THE ARMY, FACING COMBAT

LIFE AND TIMES

A very popular First Lady throughout the 1950s, Mamie Eisenhower was famous for her nice clothes, her outgoing personality, and her obvious pride in her husband. Born in Boone, Iowa, in 1896, she grew up in Denver, Colorado, with three sisters. One day in 1915 she met a young second lieutenant just out of West Point while he was on a weekend pass.

A romance was kindled, and on Valentine's Day of 1916, Dwight Eisenhower gave Mamie a miniature version of his West Point ring as a promise ring. The couple was married the following summer, and then began a typical pattern for Army wives: numerous moves throughout the United States, a couple of stints overseas, and more houses than she could remember.

Dwight rose through the Army ranks, and when World War II broke out, he was dispatched to England while Mamie stayed in Washington with their children. Eventually her husband became the supreme commander of all allied forces in Europe, and his military victories and strong character made him a hero to people the world over.

After the war, the couple purchased a home in Gettysburg, Pennsylvania (the first home they'd ever owned), and sought peace in their rural surroundings. Ike became president of Columbia University and served as commander of the North Atlantic Treaty Organization forces as politicians on both sides of the aisle began wooing him.

During the presidential campaign in 1952, Dwight Eisenhower toured the country with Mamie by his side. After having spent so much time apart due to military duties, she was happy to be able to travel with her husband.

When Ike won the election, Mamie began serving as First Lady in a world that was very different from that of her predecessors. International air travel had become common, and the Eisenhowers entertained an unprecedented number of foreign leaders and dignitaries. Mamie threw herself into the role of America's hostess, and the public perception of the First Lady changed from that of the nation's homemaker to one of America's most important ambassadors.

While her style and grace contributed to the couple's popularity, Ike's laid-back approach to government and the economic boom of the 1950s made this a golden era in U.S. history. Americans embraced both Ike and Mamie because they were strong, friendly, and down-to-earth people. Everything about them seemed to signify America's strength, from their easy manner with the press to their healthy family—John Eisenhower, their second son, followed his father's career in the Army, then became a best-selling author and eventually the United States ambassador to Belgium.

In 1961 the Eisenhowers returned to Gettysburg for eight years of contented retirement. After Ike died in 1969, Mamie continued to live on the farm, devoting her time to family and friends. Mamie passed away on November 1, 1979. She is buried beside her husband in a small chapel on the grounds of the Eisenhower Library in Abilene, Kansas.

INTERESTING FACTS

Because of Ike's career in the Army, the Eisenhowers moved an estimated thirty-three times in their fifty-three years of marriage. As a result, the White House was actually a fairly permanent home for them, since they lived there for eight years.

Mamie struggled with Ménière's disease, which caused her to struggle with vertigo, nausea, and impaired vision. She also suffered with a rheumatic heart. The First Lady needed extra rest and at times handled her duties from the comfort of her bedroom.

Mrs. Eisenhower's favorite television show was the soap opera *As the World Turns,* which she tried to watch every afternoon. She also enjoyed *I Love Lucy.* Mamie enjoyed pretty clothes and delighted in both designer ensembles and bargains from the department store. A shade of pink that she wore frequently became known as Mamie Pink.

Mamie took her role as First Lady seriously, but she did not wish to be involved in the political matters in which some First Ladies had previously shown interest. It was said that she was in her husband's office only four times during the eight years he was President.

Ike runs the country; I turn the lamb chops.

MAMIE EISENHOWER

Mamie was very busy with hostess duties, however, and greeted an average of seven hundred visitors a day during their first year in the White House. At times the White House staff found her somewhat stern, but they also noted that she never forgot anyone's birthday and seemed to genuinely care about others.

Although she declined to take on a role in the political circle, she still had impact. When she brought back the White House Easter Egg Roll, which had been absent since Franklin Roosevelt's terms, she made sure that African American children were able to join in the celebration.

To know yourself, to know that what you are doing

is right, and to live with your own conscience

is all that is necessary in life.

MAMIE EISENHOWER

Claudia Alta Taylor Johnson

1912-

This is something that I cherish. Once in a friend's home I came across this blessing, and took it down in shorthand ... it says something I like to live with: "Oh Thou, who dwellest in so many homes, possess Thyself of this. Bless the life that is sheltered here. Grant that trust and peace and comfort abide within, and that love and life and usefulness may go out from this home forever."

LADY BIRD JOHNSON

LIFE AND TIMES

Claudia Johnson spent much of her life concerned with nature and the environment, so her nickname, Lady Bird, was appropriate. Her nurse gave it to her in 1912, and her family began calling her by that name almost immediately.

When Lady Bird was just five, her mother died, so her father and an aunt, Effie Patillo, raised her. They lived in Karnack, Texas. She was a fine student with a love for clas-

118

sical literature and a head for business. She graduated from the University of Texas with a bachelor's degree in arts and journalism. Then she met a Congressional assistant by the name of Lyndon Johnson. He was working as a government secretary and was on a business trip in Texas when they met, but he promptly asked her out for a date, even though he was leaving the next day. She said no, but that didn't deter the single-minded Johnson. It is said he proposed to her the day after they met, but she turned him down.

Lyndon lived in Washington, D.C., and Lady Bird in Austin, so the couple carried on a long-distance relationship by way of letters and telegrams. Seven weeks after that first meeting, he came back to Austin and promptly proposed to her. He was surprised when she accepted, and they were married in 1934.

For the next thirty years, they would focus much of their lives on Lyndon's political career. Not satisfied with being a hostess and greeter, Lady Bird served equally well as a partner and confidante to her husband. When he volunteered for naval service during World War II, she kept his Congressional office open. When he had a heart attack and spent more than three weeks recuperating, she ran the office until he could return. Once, when asked about his wife's organizational abilities, Johnson joked that voters "would have happily elected her over me."

During the 1960 presidential campaign, Lady Bird put in more than thirty-five thousand miles on the campaign trail, and during Lyndon's term as Vice President, she visited more than thirty countries as America's ambassador of goodwill. After President Kennedy's assassination in 1963, Lyndon became President, and Lady Bird feared she could not live up to the sense of style and fashion that Jacqueline Kennedy had brought to the White House. Instead, she decided to give the President's mansion a definite Texas feel, and she began a series of dinners and barbeques that were uniquely Southwestern.

She established the First Lady's Committee for a More Beautiful Capital. Lady Bird encouraged people to participate in cleaning and beautifying the city. That spread to a Beautify America campaign, which was the beginning of America's renewed concern for a safer, cleaner environment. Lady Bird also took an active role in her husband's war on poverty program, and she helped get the Head Start program for preschool children off the ground.

Wildflowers are survivors.

Many are native to this land;

many, like us, are immigrants

who sent their descendants across the nation

on the wheels of covered wagons,

on the hooves of horses, or

in the pockets of frontier children.

LADY BIRD JOHNSON

After Lyndon Johnson had completed Kennedy's term and had been reelected, things became difficult for his administration. The unpopular war in Vietnam and significant social upheaval were terribly taxing, and Lyndon did not seek reelection. When his term ended, the couple returned to Texas. He died in 1973.

In 1970, Lady Bird wrote *White House Diary* about her life, then helped produce a documentary film about the role of the First Lady called *The First Lady: A Portrait of Lady Bird Johnson* in 1981. Both projects were filled with details that helped Americans better understand the responsibilities and pressures faced by the President's wife.

Mrs. Johnson continues to live at the Ranch in Stonewall, Texas, and she also has a house in Austin. She works with the National Wildflower Research Center and also serves on the Board of the National Geographic Society. She is a member of St. Barnabas Episcopal Church in Fredericksburg, Texas.

INTERESTING FACTS

"Bird," as her husband called her, was not married to an easygoing man. Lyndon often ordered her around in public, was high maintenance, and set the bar very high, both for himself and for his wife, when it came to fulfilling the numerous duties before them. She is to be admired for meeting his needs, caring for her daughters, and having time to do a great deal of work of her own while in the White House. Her husband said of her, "As a companion she has no equal. She's always willing to meet you more than halfway. If you want to ride and she wants to walk, she'll ride. If she wants a fire in the living room and you don't, she says sweetly, 'We'll have it some other time.'"

That's the greatest woman I have ever known. She's good and she's kind and she doesn't have a mean thought.

FORMER SPEAKER OF THE HOUSE SAM RAYBURN

Lady Bird attended St. Mary's Episcopal School for Girls in Dallas as a girl and was required to attend services both during the week and on Sunday. Throughout her life she went to church regularly and often invited her husband to join her. One story tells of Lady Bird convincing her husband to attend an Episcopal church in Virginia with her one Sunday in November of 1967. In his sermon the pastor criticized LBJ's policy in Vietnam. Afterward, Lyndon said, "Greater love hath no man than that he goes to the Episcopal church with his wife." Perhaps most impressive is the fact that she remained committed to her husband despite his dalliances. One friend said she "had the touch of velvet and the stamina of steel." It is also known that she started and ended each day with a time of devotions and Bible reading.

Lady Bird was an exceptional manager. More than two hundred thousand guests came through the White House during the five years the Johnsons were there. She had a way of charming everyone into feeling at home when she entertained. She said things like: "I'll see you tonight, if the Lord be willin' and the creek don't rise." "I look forward to that as much as to a good case of cholera." "I'm as busy as a man with one hoe and two rattlesnakes." "Y'all come back real soon, hear now!" "I find myself, as we say down home, in mighty tall cotton."

Lady Bird had three objectives for herself when LBJ became Vice President: "To help Lyndon all I can; to lend a hand to Mrs. Kennedy when she needs me; and to be a more alive me." As First Lady, she told Chief Usher J. B. West that "Anything that's done here, or needs to be done, remember this: my husband comes first, the girls come second, and I will be satisfied with what's left." And for herself, she said that she needed to make the White House a "place where Lyndon can operate productively, and to add to his operation in every way that I can, because I have never felt so much need on his part, and so much compassion on my part for him."

Thelma Catherine Ryan Nixon

1912-1993

Helping another person gives one the deepest pleasure in the world.

PAT NIXON

The one who sows sparingly will also reap sparingly, and the one who sows bountifully will also reap bountifully. Each of you must give as you have made up your mind, not reluctantly or under compulsion, for God loves a cheerful giver. And God is able to provide you with every blessing in abundance, so that by always having enough of everything, you may share abundantly in every good work.

2 CORINTHIANS 9:6–8 NRSV

LIFE AND TIMES

The daughter of an Irish immigrant miner, Pat Nixon was born Thelma Catherine Ryan on the eve of St. Patrick's Day, and her father immediately referred to her as his St. Patrick's babe. The name stuck, and she thereafter went by Pat.

Unlike many of the First Ladies, Pat's family was poor. Her mother died when she was thirteen, leaving Pat as the only woman to tend to her father and brothers. Five years later, her father passed away, and she was left on her own to find her way. Taking a job as a sales clerk in a department store, she worked her way through the University of Southern California, graduating cum laude in 1937. After graduation, she took a position teaching high school in Whittier, California.

Pat had done some movie extra roles while a student at USC, and through a friend she got involved with the Whittier Community Players. She was cast in the same play as a young man just out of law school and hoping to start his own practice—Richard Nixon. Within a short time, the couple were married.

Caring for others creates the spirit of a nation.

PAT NIXON

Nixon served in the Navy during World War II, and Pat worked for the government. Immediately after the war ended, she put her knowledge of how government works to good use, helping her husband get elected to Congress. Over the next decade she would campaign by his side as he was elected to the House, to the Senate, and as the Vice President in Dwight Eisenhower's administration.

The couple had two children, Julie and Tricia, and were kept very busy with both political and family life. Often Pat traveled with her husband to foreign countries, and she became a warm envoy for America during an often hostile time. She was able to go with her husband on his historic visit to the People's Republic of China, as well as the summit meetings in the Soviet Union aimed at reducing the world's arms supply.

J remember through all of our campaigns, whether it was a receiving line or whether it was going to a face at the airport, she was the one that always insisted on shaking that last hand, not simply because she was thinking of that vote, but because she simply could not turn down that last child or that last person.

RICHARD NIXON

In 1960 Pat worked tirelessly in her husband's unsuccessful campaign for President, repeating her efforts in 1968, when he won. As First Lady, Pat Nixon encouraged volunteerism in America and called for those who have been given much to help the less fortunate. As a woman who had grown up without many luxuries, she knew how much a little help could mean to a family that was struggling.

She has given so much to the nation and to the world.
Her only reward was to share my exile.
She deserved so much more.

RICHARD NIXON

She also spent time adding antiques and fine art to the White House and took pains to introduce Americans to a wider variety of art. Pat is perhaps best remembered for her efforts to foster diverse music and theater talent among young people. She introduced a wide audience to everything from opera to bluegrass music.

When the Watergate scandal rocked the nation, Mrs. Nixon stood by her husband with dignity. After his resignation, the two of them moved into retirement in Park Ridge, New Jersey. She died June 22, 1993, and is buried at the Richard Nixon Library in Yorba Linda, California.

INTERESTING FACTS

As First Lady, Pat began an ecumenical worship and prayer service in the East Room that brought many people to the White House each Sunday. For Pat this was a means of encouraging dialogue while also showing her support for her Christian faith. This was consistent with the Nixons' religious life, since Pat was a Methodist as a child and her husband grew up a Quaker. They never joined one particular denomination.

The White House service was consistently deeply religious and open to all levels of government workers. The fact that maids as well as Senators attended was inspirational. On occasion private citizens were also invited, if they asked for an invitation. Men such as Billy Graham, Dr. Norman Vincent Peale, and Rabbi Louis Finkelstein all led services.

My mother's faith in God sustained her during the last difficult years of her life.

TRICIA NIXON COX

For nearly twenty years, *Good Housekeeping* readers named Pat Nixon one of the ten most admired women in the world.

While her husband was Vice President, Pat accompanied him on a goodwill trip to Venezuela. The trip was a disaster. A plot to assassinate her husband was uncovered. When the Nixons' plane landed in Caracas, a small welcoming committee was overwhelmed by a mob of angry demonstrators who proceeded to spit at the Nixons and throw garbage on them. Throughout the ordeal, the press noted Pat's self-control and calm face. She even hugged a child who gave her flowers, and the press reported that in response to one young girl cursing and spitting on her, Pat leaned across a barricade to pat the offender's shoulder. It is said the young girl turned away, ashamed.

Even when people can't speak your language, they can tell if you have love in your heart.

PAT NIXON, HER EPITAPH

The situation worsened when the Vice President and the Venezuelan foreign minister took one car and Pat and the foreign minister's wife took another to their next destination. As the motorcade wound through the city, the cars were hit by rocks and even pipes and baseball bats as a mob of more than five hundred people got involved. The two women watched in horror as demonstrators tried to overturn the Vice President's car and set fire to it.

The cars were able to make a beeline for the American embassy, and after a night spent under heavy guard, the Nixons returned to the United States. Following the trip, Nixon's twelve Secret Service agents were commended by President Eisenhower for heroism.

Pat made a trip to Peru in 1970 following an earthquake in that country that killed around sixty-five thousand people and left nearly a million more homeless. As her daughter Julie wrote in *Pat Nixon: The Untold Story*: "Mother had visited combat hospitals, a leper colony, and the often impoverished institutions for the homeless, but she had never encountered such utter misery. Her response was to hug the Peruvians who gathered around her." As one Peruvian official said, after his country had softened its long stance against America: "Her coming here meant more than anything else President Nixon could have done."

Elizabeth Bloomer
Warren Ford

1918-

It doesn't matter by whose hand a life is saved. It's always the hand of God anyway.

BETTY FORD

Dear Father in Heaven, we know you can take care of him, we know you can bring him back to us. You are our leader. You are our strength. You are what life is all about. Love and love of fellow man is what we all need and depend on. . . .

MRS. FORD'S PRAYER FOR DR. MAURICE SAGE, WHO HAD COLLAPSED AT A DINNER HOSTED BY THE JEWISH NATIONAL FUND OF AMERICA FOR THREE THOUSAND PEOPLE ON JUNE 22, 1976

LIFE AND TIMES

In the history of First Ladies, Elizabeth (Betty) Ford stands out as one of the most unique. She never had a desire for the role, nor did she expect it. In fact, she and her husband were looking forward to retirement when President Nixon's Vice President, Spiro Agnew, suddenly resigned in the midst of a scandal. Nixon surprised everyone with his choice of Gerald Ford as his new Vice President, and less than a year later Mr. Nixon resigned the presidency, leaving the job in the capable hands of Gerald Ford.

It was just the sort of surprising development that seemed to happen to the vivacious Betty Ford. Raised in Grand Rapids, Michigan, she had studied dance in college and surprised her family when she announced she would make it a career. She became a member of the famous Martha Graham dance troupe in New York City, then supported herself by working as a fashion model for the John Robert Powers agency.

Returning home to Michigan, she worked as a fashion coordinator for a department store, taught dance to handicapped children, and even organized her own dance group. She married and divorced, then met a local football hero who was running for Congress. Gerald Ford was taken with the pretty, athletic dancer, and they married during the campaign.

Then thirty years of politics in Washington followed, with Jerry representing the people of Michigan and Betty taking care of the family. The couple had four children, and Betty ran their home, took on volunteer roles to set an example to others, and became a regular among the House wives and Senate wives groups. She also became a fine campaigner and excellent speaker, comfortable in a wide array of groups.

When the Fords moved into the White House, Betty wasn't thrilled with the responsibilities of being First Lady.

It was a tough time for Republicans, with the Watergate scandals so recently in the news. The lives of the President's family were under the microscope. Yet she accepted the challenge with dignity and used her new role to her advantage. With the self-confidence she'd shown as a dancer and single woman, she was able to speak openly about issues she found important, such as the Equal Rights Amendment. She is probably best remembered for her willingness to speak openly about her breast cancer and for the candid manner in which she dealt with her battle against drugs and alcohol.

I believe there's a meaning for

everyone's coming into this world,

that we're put here for a purpose and

when we've achieved that and it's time

for us to go, the Lord takes us, and nothing

can make it otherwise. I believe it,

but it's hard for the ones who are left behind.

BETTY FORD, FOLLOWING THE DEATH OF HER MOTHER

Undergoing surgery for breast cancer in 1974, she discussed her situation openly, thereby publicizing one of the biggest killers of women and no doubt helping save countless lives by encouraging women to do self-exams. When she spoke honestly on television about her battle with alcohol in 1978, it brought that issue out of the closet and got America talking frankly about alcoholism and how to treat it. Her friendliness, her honesty, and her willingness to get people

131

talking about delicate subjects have made her a model for many women, both in America and around the globe.

INTERESTING FACTS

When her husband became Minority Leader in the House in January of 1965, Betty was excited for him but soon discovered that the position took away her husband. "There followed a long stretch of time when Jerry was away from home 258 days a year. I had to bring four kids up by myself," she said. Many years later she admitted she was resentful of that time in their lives, and Jerry confirmed it put a heavy strain on their marriage.

When Gerald Ford took his oath of office as President, he honored Betty: "I am indebted to no man and only to one woman—my dear wife."

The White House was said to be significantly warmer after the Fords moved in. Betty wanted her family to be at home and endeavored to fill the place with music, laughter, and even dance. When she greeted the White House guards and there was no response, she discovered that there had been a rule in the Nixon White House that guards could not talk to the President and his wife. She quickly changed that. It was a good change, and the White House gained some much needed cheer and became a friendlier place. There were changes as well in the way visitors were entertained.

It's interesting that Betty enjoyed the White House years in part because she saw more of her husband than she ever had previously during his years in office, and also because she was able to share her opinions and causes and be herself at the same time. Though she enraged many with her liberal views, she was also greatly loved for being candid and honest.

Betty's legacy is the Betty Ford Center for Drug and Alcohol Rehabilitation, which was opened in 1982. Located in Rancho Mirage, California, it has helped thousands of people conquer their addictions, just as Betty conquered her own addiction in 1978. She once said, "I think doing constructive things and helping people is probably the best cure in the world for your personal problems."

God has allowed me—along with thousands of others—

to carry a message, a message that says,

there's help out there, and you too can be a survivor.

BETTY FORD

Rosalynn Smith Carter

1927-

What you can do is the *best* you can do. You seek guidance
from God to do what's right and best. . . . I think if you
are deeply rooted in your faith before you get there, it is
a lot easier. I was always so thankful for growing up in
the church. I don't see how anybody without faith could
maintain any kind of stability or equilibrium when those
things happen to you. I think if you do have a deep religious
faith then you just fall back on it.

ROSALYNN CARTER

LIFE AND TIMES

Born in the tiny town of Plains, Georgia, Rosalynn was
given the name Eleanor Rosalynn Smith but always went
by the name Rosalynn. When she was thirteen, her father
died and her mother began making dresses to help feed

the family. As the oldest child, Rosalynn worked beside her mother, helping with sewing, cleaning, cooking, and raising her siblings. Though poor, she decided she wanted to go to college, and she enrolled in Georgia Southwestern College in 1945.

Her best friend at college suggested Rosalynn might like to meet her brother, Jimmy Carter, a young man home from the Naval Academy. After one date, Jimmy knew he'd found the girl he was going to marry. They were wed the next year, and Jimmy's Navy career had them moving often. Each child was born in a new location: John in Virginia, James in Hawaii, Donnel in Connecticut, and Amy in Georgia. After the death of his father, Jimmy decided to leave the service and save the family business, so both Jimmy and Rosalynn got involved with managing the peanut and seed enterprise.

In 1962 Jimmy Carter won a seat in the Georgia Senate. Rosalynn found campaigning to be uncomfortable and intrusive, and once, when she was asked to give a speech, she got sick to her stomach. But over time, as her husband's political career blossomed, she became more comfortable in her role. In 1970 they moved into the Georgia statehouse, and in 1976 they campaigned for the White House. During that year, Rosalynn traveled independently back and forth across America, the first nominee's wife to essentially establish her own campaign. She became a fine speaker, and her quiet, friendly manner appealed to people tired of the usual Washington crowd. There was something small-town about Rosalynn, and her speeches about family, church, and community resonated with voters.

Rosalynn then became a hardworking First Lady, attending Cabinet meetings and major briefings with her husband and frequently representing the President at ceremonial occasions. Her style worked well with foreign leaders, and she often served as the President's personal emissary to Latin American countries.

Personally, she wanted to focus attention on the performing arts, and she expanded the tradition of inviting leading American artists to the White House. She also took a leadership role in programs aimed at helping small rural communities, those in need of mental health care, and the elderly.

Our national virtue is helping others;

our heritage is giving.

Rosalynn Carter

After their one term in office, Rosalynn Carter wrote her autobiography, *First Lady from Plains,* which offered a wonderful firsthand look at the funny and poignant things that happen in the life of a First Lady. Now she serves at the Carter Center in Atlanta, an organization that promotes peace and human rights worldwide.

Interesting Facts

Rosalynn grew up with church being a prominent part of her life. Her mother read to her from the Bible each evening, and Rosalynn attended church regularly—her grandmother was Lutheran, her grandfather was Baptist, and her parents were Methodists. After she and Jimmy were married, she became a member at the Baptist church he had grown up attending.

Early on, the Carter family supported the integration of their local churches. Jimmy's mother was a registered nurse and had a reputation in the community for her willingness to treat any patient, black or white. When the Carters completed their tenure in the White House, they returned to

Plains, Georgia, and Rosalynn picked up where she had left off. The Carters continue to be active in the community, both within their church and also working for the charities they both love.

When problems come, when you are burdened down, when you have tried everything and nothing works, release it to God. That was the key. Release! Release!

ROSALYNN CARTER

Often Rosalynn and Jimmy were seen as a team in the White House. They explained that her involvement was a natural extension of their many years together and of how they had always worked together and considered themselves "equal and full partners," with Jimmy being the one with the career and Rosalynn playing a supporting role. She was comfortable with this concept because her husband regarded her as his partner, even if the public didn't know or believe it. Since she could speak informatively on his policies, he was able to send her on diplomatic missions. He was comfortable doing this because he considered her as "an almost perfect extension of himself." One reporter who interviewed the two Carters separately said he had just met "two Jimmy Carters" after leaving the White House.

After her husband's comments to *Playboy* regarding "lusting in his heart," Rosalynn was asked if *she* had ever committed adultery. Her answer? "If I had, I wouldn't tell you!"

Rosalynn remains active in helping others. She and her husband continue to be involved in causes such as Habitat for Humanity and have gained acclaim for all they have accomplished in their years since the White House. Together they wrote the book *Everything to Gain: Making the Most of the Rest of Your Life*. Though the book was a success, they agreed never to write together again because it was, as Jimmy described it, "the worst thing we have ever been through" due to their differing writing styles. "If Rosalynn wrote something, it was sacred. It was like she just came down off Mount Sinai with it," said Jimmy. Rosalynn considered Jimmy's swiftly written chapters to be first drafts and nothing more.

Barbara Pierce Bush

1925-

I would certainly say, above all, seek God. He will come to you if you look. There is absolutely NO down side. Please expose your children and set a good example for them by going to church. We, your Dad and I, have tried to live as Christian a life as we can. We certainly have not been perfect. Maybe you can! Keep trying.

FROM A LETTER BARBARA WROTE TO HER CHILDREN
AND NEVER SENT

LIFE AND TIMES

The American people have had great affection for Barbara Bush. She claimed it was because she looked like "everyone's grandmother" with her white hair and warm manner, but she allowed that it might also have to do with her character: "I'm fair, I like children, and I love my husband." She is the type of person everyone wants in a First Lady.

Born in 1925 to the president of McCall Corporation, she had a happy and active childhood. She was sent to a boarding school in South Carolina for high school, and it was there at a Christmas dance that she met George Bush, a senior at Phillips Academy in Andover, Massachusetts. They became engaged when she was seventeen, just before he went off to war as a Navy bomber pilot. When George returned on leave, they were married.

I married the first man I ever kissed. When I tell my children that they just about throw up.

BARBARA BUSH

After the war, George graduated from Yale, and the couple moved to Texas. They had six children, and George built a career in the oil industry. From there he launched a career in public service, working as ambassador to the United Nations, chairman of the Republican National Committee, chief of the U.S. Liaison Office in the People's Republic of China, director of the Central Intelligence Agency, and eventually Vice President under Ronald Reagan. The couple moved twenty-nine times in their first forty-four years of marriage.

With George gone so often, Barbara took care of everything from fixing the home to paying the bills to disciplining the children. She was strong and outgoing and friendly, and she understood that there could be chaos in a political family. But when their daughter Robin, just three years old, died of leukemia in 1953, it changed both Barbara and George. Barbara's hair changed from the color of her youth to her trademark white that year. They both admit to becoming softer, to caring more about people who are suffering, because they've been through deep grief themselves.

Barbara was always an asset to her husband during his campaigns. Her friendly and forthright manner won her high marks from the voters and the press. As wife of the Vice President, she took on literacy as her special cause. When she became First Lady, Barbara got involved with several organizations devoted to literacy, and she founded the Barbara Bush Foundation for Family Literacy, contributing one million dollars to it from private funds.

Barbara became involved in literacy programs after her son Neil was diagnosed with dyslexia. When Barbara was in the White House, she made the most of the opportunity and brought the startling news to the American people that thirty-five million people in America couldn't read beyond the eighth-grade level. In addition, there were twenty-three million more people who were considered "functionally illiterate," meaning they could not read or write beyond the fourth-grade level. She often explained to audiences the ripple effects of illiteracy—poverty, crime, voter and civic apathy, and drug use among them.

She also became a strong voice for the homeless, the elderly, those with AIDS, and school volunteer programs.

George Bush and I have been the two luckiest people in the world, and when all the dust is settled and all the crowds are gone, the things that matter are faith, family, and friends. We have been inordinately blessed, and we know that.

BARBARA BUSH

At the time of this writing, Barbara and George Bush live in their home in Houston, Texas, where she enjoys being part of the community. Devoted to her family and still exuding warmth and humor, Barbara finds time to serve on the board of the Mayo Clinic and to continue her activism for literacy in America.

INTERESTING FACTS

Millie, the springer spaniel that was part of the Bush family during their time in the White House, was voted Washington, D.C.'s "ugliest dog." She later dictated to Barbara Bush an entire "dogobiography" of her time in the White House. The book was an immediate best seller.

Mrs. Bush was praised for her kind manner when receiving Hillary Clinton into the White House for a tour of the family quarters. This is a customary gesture, yet Barbara was especially warm in spite of the fact that her husband had been defeated. She embraced Hillary warmly and for all to see. She also left Hillary with some words of wisdom regarding the reporters crowding the South Lawn. "Avoid this crowd like the plague, and if they quote you, make . . . sure they heard you."

Never lose sight of the fact that the most important yardstick of your success will be how you treat other people—your family, friends, and coworkers, and even strangers you meet along the way.

BARBARA BUSH

Barbara was happy to have the opportunity to work for the causes she cared about, but she didn't neglect her husband.

He once said, "She'll go to bat for me, sometimes more than I'm inclined myself," when he was insulted for his policies or actions as President. Her image as a nurturing and independent woman who cares about others came through clearly when she visited children suffering with leukemia and hugged those diagnosed with AIDS. She also urged a more conciliatory approach toward gays in the Republican Party.

Hillary Diane Rodham Clinton

1947-

Do all the good you can,
by all the means you can,
in all the ways you can,
in all the places you can,
and all the times you can,
to all the people you can,
as long as ever you can.

JOHN WESLEY, OFTEN QUOTED BY HILLARY CLINTON TO EXPLAIN
WHAT HER PERSONAL FAITH REQUIRES OF HER

LIFE AND TIMES

Hillary Clinton grew up in Park Ridge, a suburb of Chicago. She was an active participant in both organized sports and her church. A natural leader, she was a member of the National Honor Society and took several student leadership positions. At Wellesley College she mixed academics with student government, then went on to law school at Yale, where she served on the board of editors for the prestigious *Yale Law Review*.

One day, while working in the library, she noticed a young man who would not stop staring at her. After a while, she simply walked up to him and said, "If you're going to keep staring at me, I might as well introduce myself." The man's name was Bill Clinton, and soon the two became almost inseparable.

After graduation Hillary advised the Children's Defense Fund and was part of the impeachment inquiry staff advising the House Judiciary Committee during the Watergate hearings. But she was in love with Bill Clinton, and she eventually decided to follow her heart and move to Arkansas to be with him. They married in 1975, and she joined the faculty of the University of Arkansas Law School that same year.

Bill was gearing up his political career, and Hillary was always an integral part of that plan. The same year her husband won the governorship of Arkansas, President Carter appointed Hillary to the board of the Legal Services Corporation.

For a dozen years she balanced family, law, and public service as the First Lady of Arkansas. She chaired the Arkansas Educational Standards Committee, co-founded the Arkansas Advocates for Children and Families, and served on the boards of the Arkansas Children's Hospital, Legal Services, and the Children's Defense Fund.

When her husband ran for the presidency, Hillary was right there beside him, and early in the years at the White House, she was his closest advisor. She chaired the Task Force on National Health Care Reform and became one of the country's leading advocates for expanding health insurance coverage and ensuring childhood immunizations. Later Hillary would write a weekly newspaper column, filled with her observations on women, children, and the people she had met in her travels around the world. Her book *It Takes a Village* became a best seller, and she won a Grammy award for her recording of it.

When things became difficult for her husband politically, Hillary stepped out on her own with outspoken criticism on the divisive nature of politics, then decided to establish her own political legacy. In November 2000, she became the first former First Lady to be elected to the United States Senate, and at the time of this writing, she serves the State of New York in that capacity.

Her name is now routinely mentioned as a prospective Democratic candidate for President in 2008 or beyond.

INTERESTING FACTS

Hillary took the position of First Lady to a new level—she claimed an office in the West Wing only a few days after her husband was inaugurated. She was immediately made head of a task force to study the feasibility of a national health care system. The country had gotten, as Bill Clinton liked to say, "two for the price of one" when he was elected President.

I am particularly indebted to the many people who taught Sunday school and vacation Bible school. I can remember the lessons there, sometimes more vividly than what I have read or seen just last week. How many times did I sing the song, "Jesus Loves the Little Children of the World." "Red and yellow, black and white, they are precious in His sight." Those words have stayed with me more personally and longer than many earnest lectures on race relations.

HILLARY RODHAM CLINTON

Early on, Hillary announced that she was to be called Hillary Rodham Clinton, which caught conservatives by surprise. During her husband's time as Governor of Arkansas from 1978 to 1980, she had gone by her maiden name. When he lost the race in 1980 and then tried again to gain the office of Governor in 1982, she began to go by her married name in an effort to appease Arkansas residents who resented her independence. Bill was reelected in November 1982.

Hillary grew up in the Methodist Church. She was deeply religious even as a young girl. She remains a committed member of that denomination to this day because of the emphasis placed on social service and personal salvation.

Hillary always carries a small Bible with her—prayer and study lead her each day as she carries out her duties as a Senator, mother, and wife. She explains that her role as a Christian requires her to "take action to alleviate suffering."

Religion is not just about one's relationship with God, but about what values flow out of that relationship, how we follow them in our daily lives and especially in our treatment of our neighbors next door and all over the world.

HILLARY RODHAM CLINTON

During the United Methodist General Conference in 1996, Hillary opened her speech with these words and delighted the crowd: "I have to confess to you that I have not been this nervous, with one hundred fifty bishops, someone told me, behind me, since I read in my home church my confirmation essay on what Jesus means to me."

Senator Hillary Rodham Clinton will hold a unique place in our nation's history—she is the first of the First Ladies to be elected to a public office. Despite intense criticism, she has stood by her family, no matter what the circumstances.

Laura Lane Welch Bush

1946-

I'd like to share with you a Psalm that has special meaning in my life and which speaks volumes to many of us during difficult times:

Psalm 46

God is our refuge and strength,
  an ever-present help in trouble.
Therefore we will not fear, though the earth give way
  and the mountains fall into the heart of the sea,
though its waters roar and foam
  and the mountains quake with their surging. Selah
There is a river whose streams make glad the city of God,
  the holy place where the Most High dwells.
God is within her, she will not fall;
  God will help her at break of day.
Nations are in uproar, kingdoms fall;
  he lifts his voice, the earth melts.
The LORD Almighty is with us;

the God of Jacob is our fortress. Selah
Come and see the works of the LORD,
the desolations he has brought on the earth.
He makes wars cease to the ends of the earth;
he breaks the bow and shatters the spear,
he burns the shields with fire.
"Be still, and know that I am God;
I will be exalted among the nations,
I will be exalted in the earth."
The LORD Almighty is with us;
the God of Jacob is our fortress. Selah

These words give us hope and confidence by reminding us of God's infinite strength. My husband and I find strength in the word of the Lord, and we realize the power that prayer has in our own lives.

LAURA BUSH, INTRODUCTORY REMARKS,
NATIONAL DAY OF PRAYER, MAY 2002

LIFE AND TIMES

Laura Bush was born on November 4, 1946, in Midland, Texas. Inspired by her second grade teacher, Laura decided she would also become a schoolteacher and earned a degree in education from Southern Methodist University in 1968. She then taught elementary school in Dallas and Houston before earning a master's degree in library science from the University of Texas. While working as a public school librarian in Austin, she met and married George Walker Bush in 1977.

As the role of the First Lady has evolved, it has included a commitment to some specific area of need in our country. Like other contemporary First Ladies, Laura Bush has a cause. She is particularly interested in advancing education and has created a national initiative called Ready to Read, Ready to Learn that helps parents recognize the importance of reading aloud to their children. She has also helped develop a series of magazines that provide parents with helpful information about their children's health and intellectual development.

Not long after becoming First Lady, Laura convened a White House Summit on Early Childhood Cognitive Development and has hosted several regional summits around the country, with the focus on teaching children to read and love books. Laura has said several times that her goal is to ensure that all children learn to read by the third grade. A childhood love for Nancy Drew mysteries fostered Laura's lifelong passion for reading.

In September 2001 Mrs. Bush joined with the Library of Congress to launch the first National Book Festival in Washington, D.C. She also hosts the White House Salute to America's Authors to celebrate our country's great literary works. As a longtime teacher, Laura Bush has seen the value of working with teacher recruitment programs, such as Teach for America, the New Teacher Project, and Troops to Teachers, which encourage students, professionals, and retired members of the military to become teachers.

A strong advocate for women's rights, Laura has spearheaded efforts to bring education to people worldwide, especially to girls. She is the only First Lady in history to give a presidential radio address, speaking out on the plight of women and children living under the Taliban. She even led an effort to build a teacher training institute for women in Afghanistan.

In honor of her mother, a breast cancer survivor, the First Lady has supported education campaigns for breast cancer and heart disease, partnering with organizations, such as the National Heart, Lung and Blood Institute, to spread the message that heart disease is the leading cause of death among women in America. Laura educates women about their risks and stresses the importance of healthy eating, exercise, and preventive screenings.

151

Laura Bush's favorite role is that of mother—the Bushes are the parents of twin daughters, Barbara and Jenna, who are named for their grandmothers.

Interesting Facts

Laura was called "Comforter-in-Chief" by *US* magazine, and her father-in-law described her once as "very strong in a quiet kind of way." Laura has commented that her relationship with her husband is "very sustaining" and that "it's always been that way, and we're lucky to have that relationship."

When Laura was just seventeen years old, she suffered a tragic experience. She was driving with some friends on a rural road and ran a stop sign before her car broadsided another vehicle in the intersection. The driver of the other car died at the scene of the accident, and more tragically, he was a close friend of Laura. For many years she struggled with guilt; in time, though, she has found both peace and forgiveness. Her life, however, was forever changed.

A hiking and camping enthusiast, Laura enjoys the great outdoors. She helped to start Preserve America, a national preservation initiative to protect our cultural and natural heritage. She highlights preservation efforts across the country and encourages Americans to get in-volved in preserving main streets, parks, and community treasures. Also Mrs. Bush replanted native grasses at the family's ranch in Crawford to preserve the beautiful Texas landscape.

Once when Laura did not attend an event with the President, he responded to a question about her absence with: "It's been raining, so she needs to sweep the porch, because the President of China is coming tomorrow." The next day, when asked if she appreciated the remark, she shook her head and mouthed, "No."

Millions of Americans seek guidance every day in prayer. I'm one of them. I also know that many Americans remember President Bush and me in their prayers, and we are grateful. I'm blessed to be married to a man who is strong enough to bear great burdens and humble enough to ask God for help. We draw on our faith in times of joy and also in times of uncertainty.

LAURA BUSH, NEW YORK TENTH ANNIVERSARY
PRAYER BREAKFAST, MAY 11, 2004

Bibliography and Sources

The American President website: www.americanpresident. org.

Anthony, Carl Sferrazza. *The Saga of the Presidents' Wives and Their Power, 1961–1990*. Vol. 2 of *First Ladies*. New York: William Morrow and Company, Inc., 1991.

Boller, Paul F. Jr. *Presidential Wives: An Anecdotal History.* New York: Oxford University Press, 1988.

Calvin Coolidge website: www.calvin-coolidge.org.

Heckler-Feltz, Cheryl. *Heart and Soul of the Nation: How the Spirituality of Our First Ladies Changed America*. New York: Doubleday, 1997.

National First Ladies' Library website: www.firstladies.org.

Parsons, Lynn Hudson. "Abigail Smith Adams," in *American First Ladies: Their Lives and Their Legacy*. 2nd ed. Edited by Lewis L. Gould. New York: Routledge, 2001.

"Quotations from the First Ladies" website: www.ci.cerritos. ca.us/library/quotations.html.

Rutherford B. Hayes Presidential Center website: www.rb hayes.org/hayes.

Schneider, Dorothy, and Carl J. Schneider. *First Ladies: A Biographical Dictionary*. New York: Checkmark Books, 2001.

Tennant, Sue E. *Prayer, Power and Petticoats: Lessons in Faith from the First Ladies from Martha Washington to Laura Bush.* Gainesville, FL: Bridge-Logos, 2004.

Watson, Robert P. *First Ladies of the United States: A Biographical Dictionary.* Boulder, CO: Lynne Rienner, 2001.

The White House website: www.whitehouse.gov

Whitton, Mary Ormsbee. *First First Ladies 1789–1865: A Study of the Wives of the Early Presidents.* New York: Hastings House, 1948.

Jerry Chip MacGregor is an associate publisher with Time Warner Book Group and the author of several books. A former pastor and college professor, he lives in Tennessee with his wife.

Marie Prys, a graduate of Dordt College, is a freelance editor and writer who works with Christian authors and publishers. She lives in the Pacific Northwest with her husband and two children.